Joining
the
ABC

**How and why handwriting & spelling
should be taught together**

Joining the ABC

How and why handwriting & spelling
should be taught together

Charles Cripps
Robin Cox

The Authors

Charles Cripps is a tutor at the Cambridge Institute of Education and runs courses for teachers of children with learning difficulties in mainstream schools. He lectures nationally and internationally on the teaching of spelling and his publications for L.D.A. include *The Stile Spelling Programme* and *A Hand For Spelling*.

Robin Cox is a primary adviser for SCS schools (North West Europe) and was previously a headteacher with SCEA in Singapore, Hong Kong, and North West Europe.

Joining the ABC
LD896
ISBN 0 905 114 72 8
© Charles Cripps & Robin Cox
First published 1989
Reprinted 1990

L.D.A., Duke Street, Wisbech, Cambs, PF'3 2AE, England.
Printed in Great Britain by
Ebenezer Baylis & Son Ltd,
The Trinity Press, Worcester, and London.

Foreword

Joining the ABC is based on the evidence of how a number of schools in the UK and Service Children's Schools, West Germany, handled the innovation of teaching joined writing from the beginning. The intention of this book is to help other schools and teachers who also are considering the teaching of joined writing to children on school entry. It is for those teachers who see that the practice of breaking up the letter formation process into 'easy' stages of - first, ball and stick letters, then adding a joining flick, and last, learning a complete joined cursive - is unnecessarily laborious.

A major part of this book is also concerned with how the teaching of joined writing influences the catching of spelling. From observational evidence, and from comments from teachers and, more importantly, children, it is clear that children do become more confident and more aware of the structure of words, and so are able to write with speed, legibility and enthusiasm from a very early age. This supports Gray's (1977) argument that 'the teaching of print should be abandoned' for young children on school entry.

In terms of the National Curriculum this book is timely, for it is very disturbing that some of the proposals in the DES document 'English for Ages 5 to 11' (1988) in the matter of spelling and handwriting, are not as forward looking as teachers had hoped. The targets too, give rise for concern. For example, one of the attainment targets is correct spelling and legible handwriting, yet the means by which this target is to be attained are largely ignored. It is hoped that this book will help to redress the balance.

Surprisingly, the UK is one of the few countries that does not have a national handwriting policy. Most Australian states and also New Zealand have, since 1984, established theirs. The United States of America, like us, has no national policy, and we are all aware of the recent concern in that country about literacy levels. Handwriting is an extremely important sub-skill and it is essential that sound policies at both primary and secondary levels are established.

Finally, the authors should like to take this opportunity of thanking Jo Finch for the idea of using snakes as an aid to correct letter formation and Julie Warrington for some of the art work in the first section of this book. The authors also wish to thank all of the teachers and particularly the children who gave so generously of their time and energy, for without them the ideas contained in this book would not have been possible. Although neither the schools nor the teachers are named throughout the book, the presented evidence is the result of the work in the following schools:

Service Children's School, West Germany

The Andrew Humphrey Primary School
Bielefeld Primary School
Bunde Primary School
Hameln Primary School
Hastenbeck Primary School
Hildesheim Primary School

UK

Bentley VCP School, Ipswich, Suffolk
Furness Vale County Primary School, Stockport, Derbyshire
St Pancras RC VAP School, Ipswich, Suffolk
Wroxham School, Wroxham Gardens, Potters Bar, Hertfordshire

Contents

1

An historical overview

Cave man 20 000 BC

It is generally believed that the beginnings of a visible and tangible form of communication are to be found in the primitive pictures drawn by cave men. The prehistoric paintings of bulls, bison, horses, and other animals of the last Ice Age, which were drawn on cave walls in Southern Europe, are thought to have served a purpose other than merely satisfying the artistic desires of man, in that they depict fertility rights and methods of hunting. However, it is only as a result of work in the 1970s by Alexander Marshack, a Research Assistant of Harvard University's Peabody Museum, that Ice Age man is now thought to have had the powers of a more formal means of communication.

Marshack, using techniques of microscopic examination and infra-red and ultraviolet photography, pointed the way to profound new insights into the life and cultural development of Ice Age man. In his article, *Exploring the Mind of Ice Age Man*, written in 1975 for the National Geographic Society's official journal, Marshack reveals his belief that the series of marks that were made with many different tools on the surface of a carved reindeer bone during the late Ice Age were 'the earliest known human notation, made more than twenty thousand years before the development of writing, arithmetic, or the calendars of later cultures we regard as civilized'. This bone notebook, commonly known as the Blanchard bone, was fashioned and carved over a considerable period to record the important sequence of the changing moon and the passing seasons (see Fig. 1). Marshack refutes the early theories that the carvings were merely decorative with the discovery that the 'author' changed the engraving stroke or toll point 24 times to make 69 marks. Some marks were gouged from left to right, some from right to left, and others in short arcs or jabbed straight in. All of these marks, which were made in a serpentine path, are not just literal images, he argues, but a complex notation of the passage of two and a quarter lunar months.

Marshack's later studies, based in SW France, of the seemingly random scribbles occurring on rocks in caves inhabited by Ice Age Man, further indicate that Cro-Magnon man was more than an artist who was doodling, he was 'slowly accumulating or building up an image which was intentional, cumulative and sequential'.

Figure 1
The markings on the Blanchard Stone
Adapted from Marshack (1975)

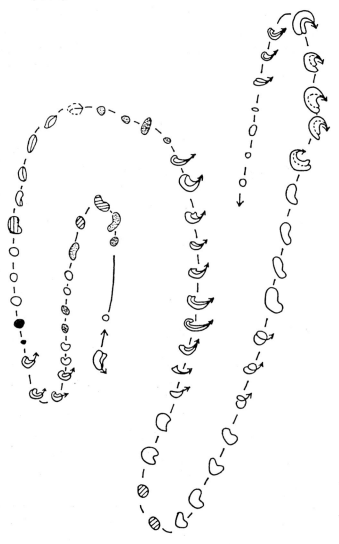

Sumerian 3000 BC

The more traditional view about the earliest form of writing is that the Sumerian civilisation, cradled in between the rivers Euphrates and Tigris at the head of the Persian Gulf, established a full system of writing in the middle of the third millenium BC. Living in productive farmlands, the Sumerians sought a practical system for setting down records of their agricultural output. The task of record-keeping fell to the priests, who collected taxes and administered the temples in the city states.

The marshes and swamps, once irrigated, left abundant alluvial silt, handfuls of which, when shaped and dried, made ideal 'notebooks'. These tablets were then scratched to make signs. However, the scratches were found to be rather fragile and easily worn away, so wedge-shaped strokes were made by pressing down on the soft clay with the triangular end of reeds. This writing, changing from a curved to a linear form, is called 'cuneiform' from

Figure 2
Some examples of early writing
Adapted from Skipp (1967)

	Pictograph	Pictograph in the position of Cuneiform	Early Cuneiform	Akkadian
To stand, to go	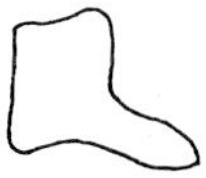		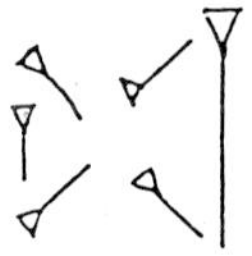	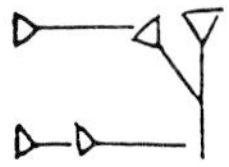
Fish	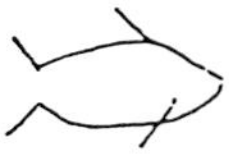		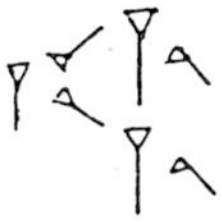	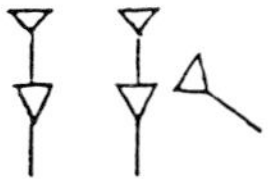
Heaven, God				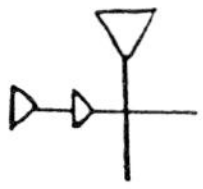
Ox		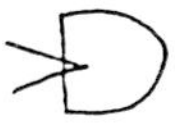	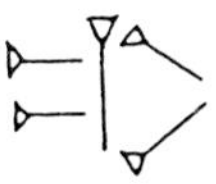	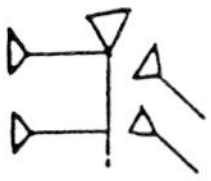
Grain			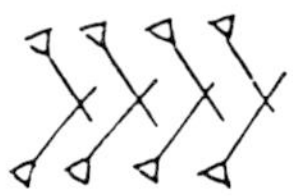	

the Latin word *cuneus* meaning 'wedge' (see Fig. 2).

When baked or dried in the hot sun, these tablets of clay were durable. Very many thousands have been discovered in good condition and can be read by scholars. Initially, standardised and stylised pictures of familiar objects, animals, etc. were used. Slowly, over a long period of years, these pictographs evolved into syllabic signs based on sound. These phonetic ideas, known as phonograms, were used in trade and thus spread to neighbouring peoples such as the Hittites and Persians.

Later, the need to adapt the phonetic syllables to a foreign language gave impetus to their further development. Akkadian became the world's first international language. It was widely used for letters and dispatches, as is particularly shown in the El-Armarna correspondence. However, the reading and writing of Sumerian and Akkadian remained so difficult that it demanded long years of scribal training. Phonetic syllables were adopted but the ideograms from which they originated remained in use (see Fig. 3). As a result, although the Mesopotamian civilisation as a whole could be classed as highly literate, the majority of people could not read nor write. Even high officials and royal personages were illiterate.

The teaching of writing in these times, which was only to boys, was the responsibility of the priests. These scribes took lessons in the temples and used the first known pupils' copybooks. The writing was pressed into the damp clay, with the teacher's writing on one side and the child's attempts on the other.

Figure 3
Adapted from Oates (1979)

Uruk IV C.3100	Sumerian C. 2500	Old Babylonian C. 1800	Neo-Babylonian C. 600 BC	Sumerian Babylonian
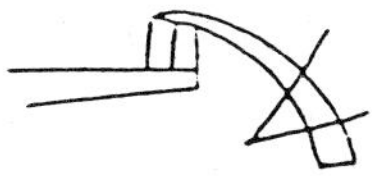		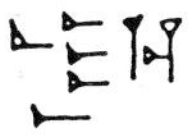	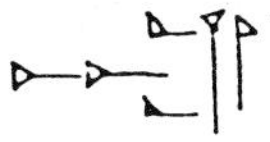	**Apin** **epinnu** *plough*
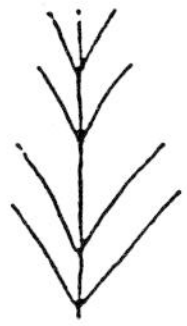	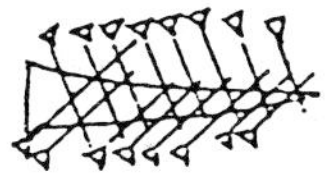	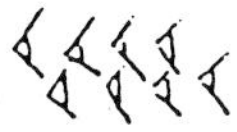	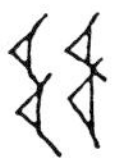	**še** **še'u** *grain*
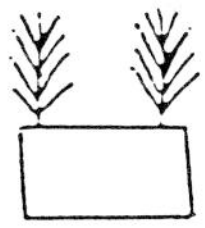	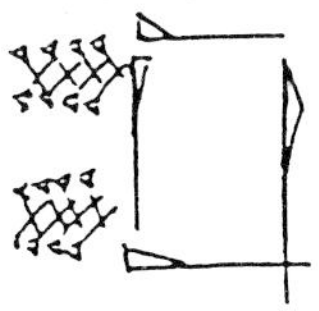			**Šar** **kirû** *orchard*
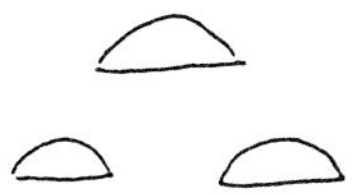				**Kur** **šadû** *mountain*
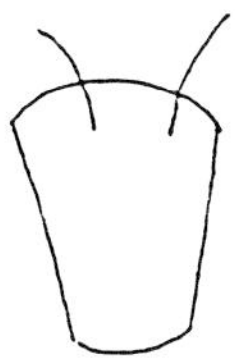	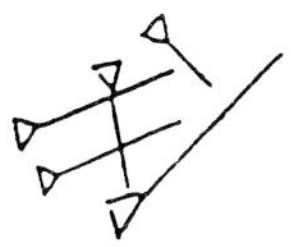	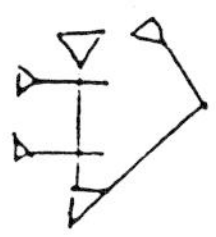	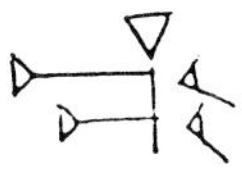	**Gud** **alpu** *ox*
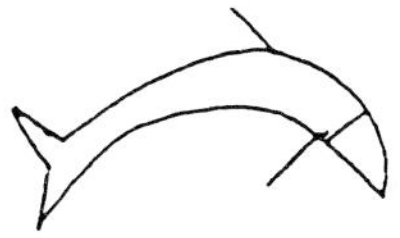	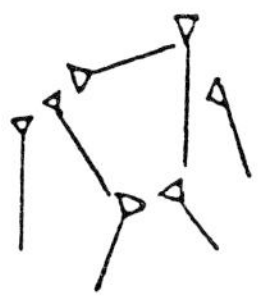		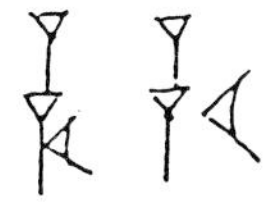	**Ku(a)** **nunu** *fish*

5

Egyptian hieroglyphs

This writing style began in SW Asia and was later introduced to the Nile valley, where the Egyptians had been using the hieroglyphic style principally for sacred inscriptions on buildings and monuments. These signs, either carved in stone or painted, included formalised pictures of people, animals, birds, household articles, tools, etc., and had been used and little changed for a period of 3000 years down to Roman times. The hieroglyphic style made use of pictograms, ideograms (which were pictures representing ideas, actions and associations), phonograms, and other signs, known as determinatives, which were added to basic signs and helped to fix the meaning.

A significant step forward from this fairly limited and clumsy form of writing came with the use of papyrus, which was made from the pith of reeds and was written on by brush or reed pen. Thus a more rapid style evolved, with the fluency eliminating the laborious pictorial quality of hieroglyphics. Twenty-four signs representing sounds were eventually used alongside a blend of ideograms and phonetic signs (see Fig. 4). Again, teaching was restricted to the few privileged boys who were training to become priests. In fact the word hieroglyphic means 'the secret writing of the priests'. The word *clericus* came to mean someone who could write, and even today we still refer to priests as clerics.

Figure 4
The Egyptian sound signs
Adapted from Skipp (1967)

Figure 4 — The Egyptian sound signs (Adapted from Skipp (1967))

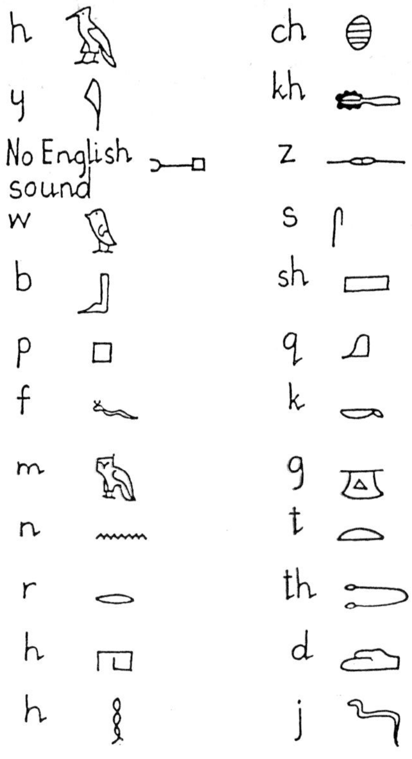

The development of the alphabet

Who actually created the alphabet remains a mystery at present. It is clear, however, that the Phoenicians, heavily influenced by Egyptian writing, quickly absorbed this next stage in the writing process into their own language early in the second millennium BC. Each of the 22 letters, none being a vowel was given a name and placed in a certain order (see Fig. 5). The first two signs of the Phoenician alphabet were named *aleph*, which meant 'ox', and *beth* which meant 'house'. The Greeks adopted this alphabet about 1000 BC and added vowels. They called the first two letters *alpha* and *beta* and from these names, which have

Figure 5
Example of early Phoenician writing
Taken from Gelb (1952)

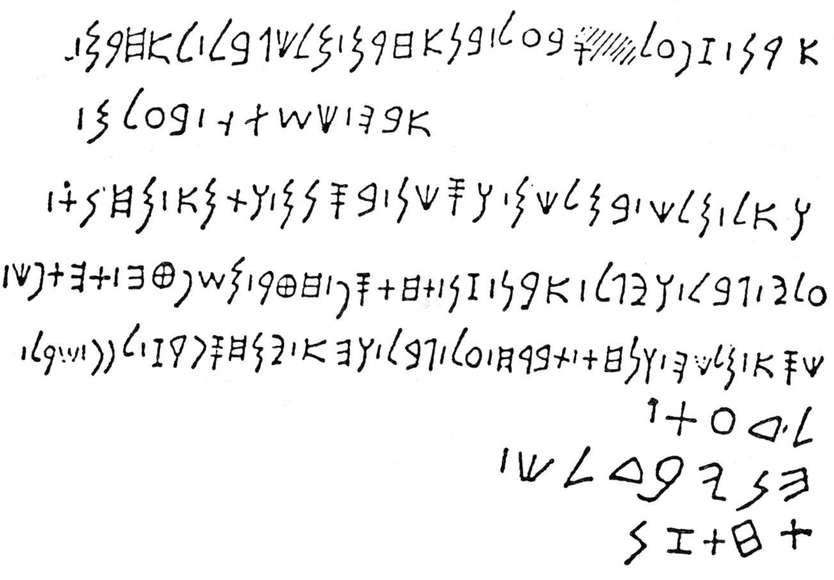

no other meaning in Greek, we have the word 'alphabet'.

At the time of the Roman Republic, some 500 years later, 22 letters were in use. The letters A B E Z I K M N O T X Y were taken over from the Greek language with hardly any change, other symbols were remodelled and adapted to make the letters C G L S P R D, and the letters V F Q were taken from letters that had become obsolete in Greek. After their early beginnings, both Greek and Latin carved inscriptions show an increasing confidence and elegance in execution and design.

Through the growth of the Roman Empire and the spread of Christianity to Europe, more systems of communication became necessary. Books, letters, orders, legal documents and records multiplied in number. The Romans were responsible for the first mass-produced books. An educated scribe, seated on a high chair, would read aloud a manuscript while one hundred slaves and scribes wrote down what he dictated and so produced one hundred copies simultaneously. This widening of interest in writing produced modifications. By the third century BC, scribes were in possession of a quickly written, cursive alphabet which had developed from the more formal shapes of the capital letters (see Fig. 6).

Figure 6
How some Roman capitals changed their shapes as a result of being copied by hand over centuries
Taken from Jarman (1979)

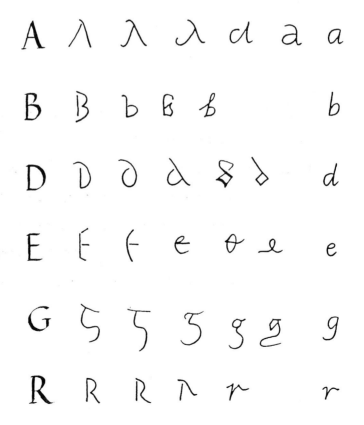

Europe 500-1800

When the only means of reproducing books was by the laborious process of copying every letter and word by hand, and when the copyists themselves were often deficient in their knowledge of Latin and other languages, it was inevitable that texts would become inaccurate. The process of replicating mistakes - even copying annotated comments in margins as if they were the original script - led to a great deal of confusion. The Emperor Charlemagne, who by conquest had united almost all of the Christian lands of western Europe, instigated the massive task of putting right the effects of centuries of neglect and confusion in the copying of texts of every kind. He insisted that all new texts, whether of the classical works of history, philosophy, grammar and poetry, treatises on science, mathematics and law, or the gospels themselves, were to be 'correct', 'uniform' and 'well-edited'. The great scholars of the day who were charged with this work developed the Carolingian minuscule, a small script of remarkable clarity and simplicity which became readily accepted throughout Charlemagne's dominion (see Fig. 7). The word minuscule can be translated as 'lower case'. From this minuscule other European styles developed but the Carolingian strain represents a standard of simplicity and beauty against which all other

Figure 7
Carolingian minuscule (ninth century)
Taken from Fairbank (1970)

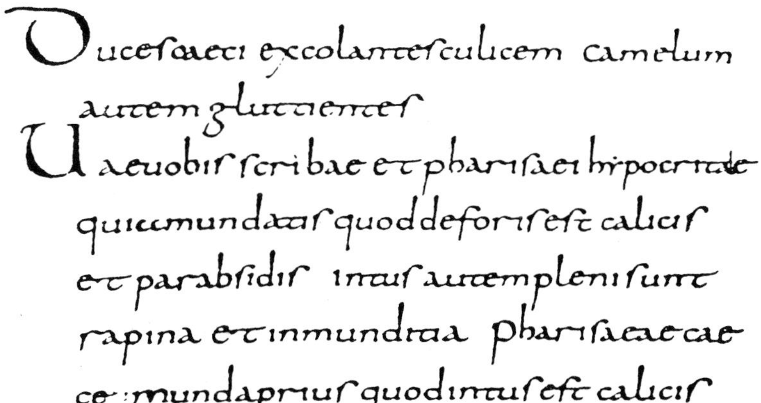

writing styles may be measured.

The rounded and separately formed Carolingian letters became subject to cursive tendencies in the interest of speed and economy. Before long, this became accepted as a style in its own right. The italic hand developed during the Italian Renaissance. A certain Niccolo Niccoli adapted the accepted classic Carolingian style by using diagonal joins. By the early

Figure 8
Italic script of Niccolo Niccoli
Taken from Fairbank (1970)

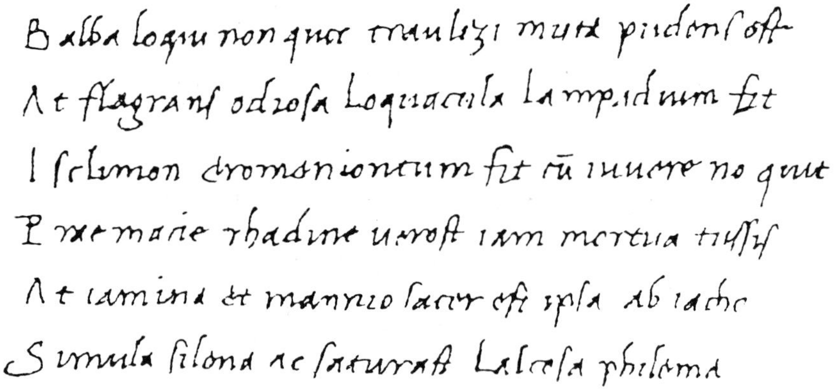

sixteenth century, a well-developed italic style was created (see Fig. 8).

It is also generally believed that during the fifteenth century Pope Eugenius IV decreed that all papal briefs be written in the style outlined by his chief scribe in *La Operina*, now

Figure 9
From La Operina
Taken from Fairbank (1970)

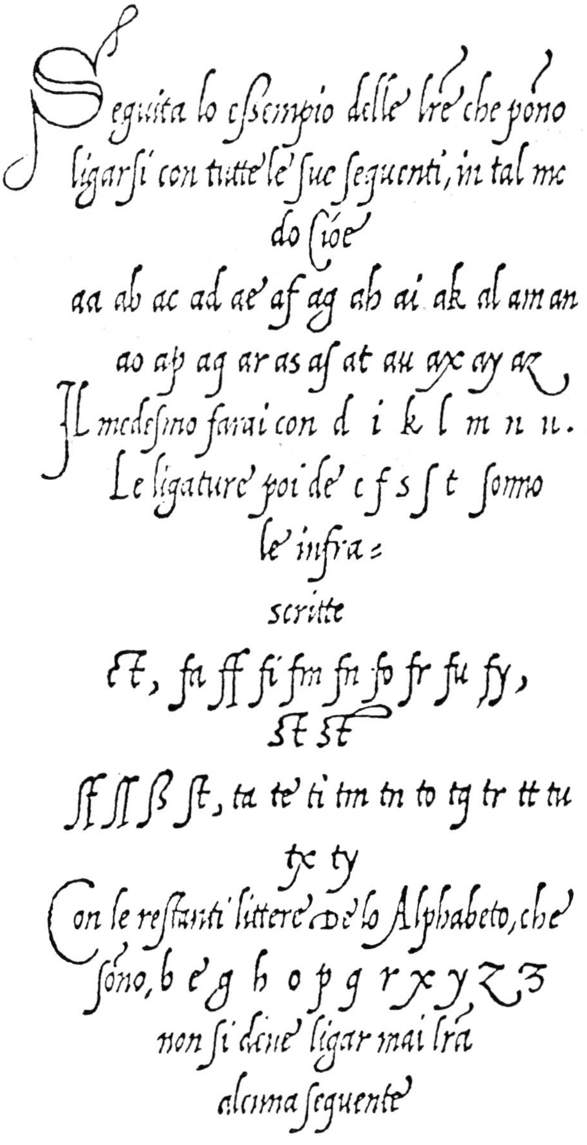

Seguita lo essempio delle lre che pono
ligarsi con tutte le sue seguenti, in tal me
do cioe

aa ab ac ad ae af ag ah ai ak al am an

ao ap aq ar as af at au ax ay az
Il medesimo farai con d i k l m n u.
Le ligature poi de c f s ſ t sonno
le infra:

scritte

ct, fa ff fi fm fn fo fr fu fy,
ſt ſt

ſf ſl ſß ſt, ta te ti tm tn to tg tr tt tu
te ty
Con le restanti littere de lo Alphabeto, che
sono, b e g h o p q r x y z z
non si dene ligar mai lra
alcuna seguente

known as the *First Writing Book* (see Fig. 9).

The invention of printing in the mid-fifteenth century resulted in the mass mechanical production of 'writing', which led to a more extensive use of the pen. In fact the first writing book to be printed and published in England in 1570, entitled *A Book Containing Divers Sortes of Hands*, set out various scripts in use. A new demand for education brought about the foundation of many schools. Copybooks were engraved and printed with instructions on lettering and how to hold a pen. The art of writing became a central part of the curriculum, with much emphasis placed on style and neatness.

The models in the earliest printed copybooks were reproduced by using engraved woodblocks. These were later replaced by metal plates. The latter method of reproduction, coupled with changing tastes, modified the style of the italic hand through the tools and methods that were involved in engraving the metal plates. The writing masters were quick to seize upon the possibilities offered by the ability to score a copper plate with a pointed steel pen and then, after making the plate, to print the result. Loops in ascenders and descenders appeared in writing models. Ultimately, during the seventeenth century, the aim was to write words, without pen lifts, in one continuous line. Many calligraphers produced a style with excessive flourishes, which was not conducive to easy copying, but beneath this extravagance lay a simple, useful and practicable cursive hand which became known as the copperplate style.

As British trade grew, more people needed to write. Many copybooks were produced, the most notable being George Bickham's *The Universal Penman*, issued in 1741.

United Kingdom 1800-today

Many tutors in the art of handwriting developed their own ideal style during the nineteenth century. Although they all worked on the principle of continuous flow, as demanded by the copperplate style, a selection of styles was produced (see Fig. 10). Copperplate was evident

Figure 10
Examples of copperplate hands
Taken from Fairbank (1970)

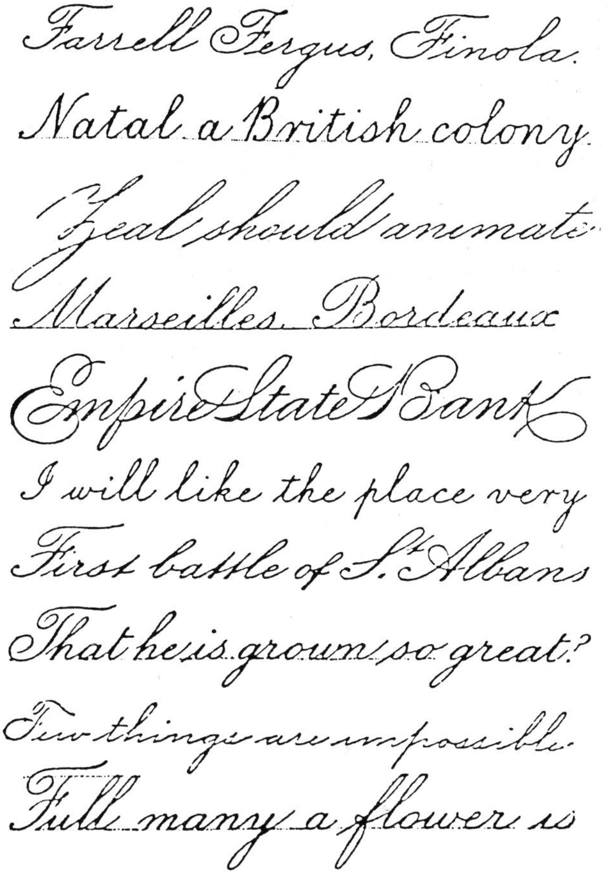

Farrell Fergus, Finola.
Natal a British colony.
Zeal should animate
Marseilles. Bordeaux
Empire State Bank
I will like the place very
First battle of S.t Albans
That he is grown so great?
Few things are impossible.
Full many a flower is

in the church schools when Her Majesty's Inspectors began to visit them in 1839. It was later taken into the curriculum of the elementary board schools in 1870, as being able to write a legible business hand, based on copperplate, was considered to be essential. One can imagine a teacher of the time writing from the copybook on the blackboard. Rows of pupils would sit silently as the teacher wrote flowingly with the chalk being lifted only at the end of the word. At other times, the pupils would labour over their copybooks, copying accurately each letter, and always beginning at the base. First they used chalk and slates and then they progressed to spluttering steel nibs on paper. Meanwhile the teacher would stride up and down between the rows, correcting pen hold, posture, and style. Left-handers were forbidden. The teacher knew very well how to instruct in penmanship and many children, in spite of the threats and harsh environment, learned copperplate handwriting and took a pride in their achievement.

In 1913 Edward Johnston, a student of old manuscripts and penmanship for fifteen years, was asked to address a conference of London teachers after he had reviewed about 30 existing copybooks and assessed their suitability for use with pupils in school. In fact he rejected them all and demonstrated instead a skeletal alphabet which included the essential shapes of the Roman alphabet (see Fig. 11). He argued that this simple form, by eliminating

Figure 11
The alphabet in print script
Taken from Jarman (1979)

abcdefg
hijklmn
opqrst
uvwxyz

the complexities in other styles, would aid the teaching of beginners to write. He also suggested that this style, now known as print script, would be helpful because it was close to the print found in reading matter.

Print script was trialled in London schools in 1916. In 1922 the Board of Education pamphlet, *Print-script*, was published. The approach soon spread far and wide, even finding favour in the United States of America where it was introduced by Miss Marjorie Wise as 'manuscript writing'. Myers (1983), however, points out that Johnston 'did not wish it to be thought that he was directly responsible for the print script characters, since he was not consulted in the experiments'. Nevertheless, regardless of origin, the influence of print script remains today in the initial teaching of handwriting in the majority of schools in the United Kingdom and some say that is the cause of many of the handwriting problems currently evident.

Not everyone accepted the print script approach. The most notable dissenter was Marion Richardson who, in 1935, produced her publication, *Writing and Writing Patterns*. She had noted that the staccato movements of some of the italic styles were inhibiting the natural flowing development required for cursive handwriting. Print script in particular did not

Figure 12
Marion Richardson alphabet

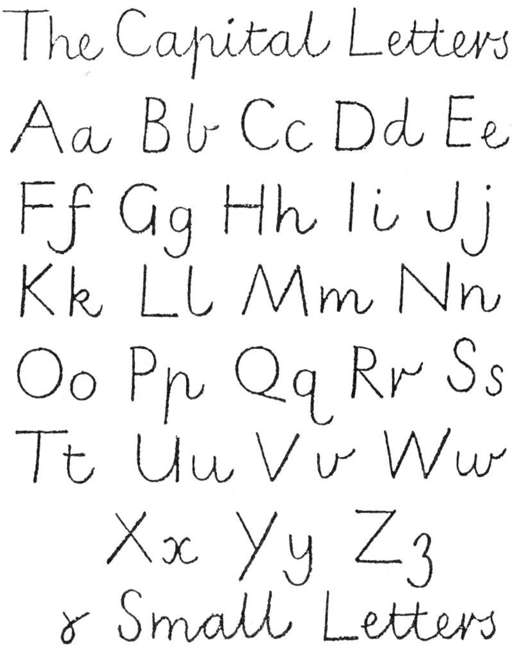

The Capital Letters
Aa Bb Cc Dd Ee
Ff Gg Hh Ii Jj
Kk Ll Mm Nn
Oo Pp Qq Rr Ss
Tt Uu Vv Ww
Xx Yy Zz
& Small Letters

lead naturally to a cursive hand. She therefore provided children with large sheets of paper and thick, soft pencils and crayons, and gave them writing patterns to follow which encouraged 'rhythm and swing'. She selected six basic patterns as being natural to the movements of a child and advocated regular practice at all stages in writing. The proposed letter shapes (see Fig. 12) were to be used throughout the child's writing development, thus avoiding the change in style from a print to a joined script. She avoided the profusion of loops and whorls that had crept in and reverted to the older, simpler style of writing, based on the Roman alphabet. The letters were wide in proportion to their height, well rounded and basically upright. In contrast to print script, many of the down strokes ended with a curve at the foot so that they led naturally to the following letter. The most obvious characteristic was the open bowl of the lower case 'b' and 'p'.

Critics of her scheme point to some poor letter formation and a propensity to produce a sprawling, widely spaced style. Strongly counterbalancing those negatives, however, is the evidence that, under pressure of speed writing, the letters deteriorate less than those of several other modern styles (Stanton 1986). Richardson was supported in 1958 by D E Fletcher who, in his manual *Quick and Legible Handwriting*, made the following comment on the use of a print script:

> 'Teachers in infant schools who, for one reason or another, may hesitate to change from the print script they have been using for so long, may be prepared to re-examine the letter shapes they have been teaching and follow the development of these shapes right through to the adult stage. From such an observation it would appear that the basic letter shapes used in print script - shapes which make use of the circle and straight line - do not lend themselves to speed and legibility. Adults will find it necessary at some stage to discard these shapes and in their place substitute a style of handwriting more likely to meet this particular requirement.'

He continues:

> 'By making use of very simple joins from the beginning, children experience the essentially cursive nature of handwriting in the very first things they write, and also they avoid having to make a changeover at the Junior level from the round upright letters of print script to the joined letter of cursive script.'

The problems of being introduced to print script in the initial stages of writing and then of having to learn to write all over again, when the joined and cursive form is introduced, were further highlighted by Robin Tanner in his contribution to the Ministry of Education's pamphlet, *Primary Education*, published in 1959.

Sadly, sixteen years later, the Bullock Report (1975) did not address the debate in a forthright manner at all. Indeed, the committee decided to 'sit on the fence' by stating the argument clearly but without making a comment:

> 'One question on which opposing views are often expressed is that of the kind of handwriting with which children should begin in the infant school. Some teachers

believe that print script should be used and that this should be as near in appearance as possible to the type face of the child's first books, so that he will have fewer characters to learn. There is certainly economy in using the same alphabet for both reading and writing, but the opponents of print script contend that it ignores a fundamental requirement of handwriting - a continuous linear, rhythmic movement. They observe that many children do not find it easy to change later to a cursive script.'

Teachers were given no guidance as to the best approach. Nicolette Gray refuelled the debate in the article, 'Laying down the Letter', which appeared in the *Times Educational Supplement* in 1977. Gray had been charged with research, for the Inner London Education Authority, into the need for a new handwriting model. In her article she expressed concern about the need for children to relearn letters and write 'joined up' writing after two years of learning a print script. Were children, she asked, seeing joined up writing 'simply as print script with joins added'? She concluded that:

'Cursive writing, if it is to be well formed, enjoyable, or even legible, must be recognised as having its own proper forms and beauty, related to the way the human hand moves. ... [Print] is not only a perverse way of starting to write, but one which actively inhibits formation of a good hand at a later stage. It should be abandoned.'

Gray's strong conclusions were perhaps influenced by a seminar of the Association Typographique Internationale, held at the University of Reading in 1976, where reports were received on the state of handwriting in twelve countries. Sweden was the only country with a clear national policy. All of the other countries which were represented were in a state of flux, expressing a variety of different views on the question of new models for handwriting. Whilst this debate has been developing, the actual teaching of the skill of handwriting has been on the decline.

During the 1930s, and following the Second World War, a new emphasis on free expression and creativity began to influence the primary schools. There was a rebellion against the repetitive and boring nature of working from copybooks. With the encourage-ment of more imaginative writing and with the advent of grouping children and of teaching an integrated day, correspondingly less emphasis was placed on the formal teaching of handwriting.

Prue Wallis Myers, in her article 'Handwriting in English Education' which was written for *Visible Language* (1983), sums up the approach that was encouraged by many:

'Handwriting was thought of at the early infant stage as the clue which relates talking with reading. The young child watched his teacher write his talk. She does this in his drawing book under his picture, which he describes to her. Then, while she attends to the next child, he takes the book away, sits down and tries to imitate the peculiar thing he saw his teacher doing - those queer marks he saw her making. But he cannot remember how the symbols were made, for she went too quickly and made too many at once. So first he uses his eyes to register a mark, then he uses his pencil to try to represent it, by pulling the pencil round and about, sometimes making lines grow up from the bottom. He plays a kind of matching game as he copies, but something else happens. As the letter shapes recur, he finds himself repeating certain gymnastics with his pencil, until the eye dictates directly through the mind to the hand how to respond when he sees a certain letter to copy. Thus, writing habits are acquired by eye, hand and mind, before the child has been directly taught how to make letters. This is the wrong way round, for it is the movements that make the letter shapes. When the teacher comes round later to inspect the child's work, the marks representing the letters are hardly legible.'

Myers concludes by decrying this approach to 'creative writing' which eliminated the time needed to be set aside for teaching competency in letter formation. The final demise of handwriting, she recalls, was when the Plowden Report (1967) made such scant mention of the skill that it did not warrant an entry in the index.

In the latter part of the twentieth century, the physical skill of handwriting is coming under renewed threat. It could be argued that the increasing popularity of the typewriter and, more recently, of the word processor will eliminate the need to communicate through the form of handwriting. Modern technology cannot and should not be resisted but there is still a need for the modern pupil to learn how to write fluently, legibly, and with speed.

The Bullock Report (1975), as mentioned earlier, gave only a cursory glance at the teaching of handwriting. However, the committee, after questioning teachers as to the amount of time spent on the activity by 6 and 9-year old children, did have this to say about the neglect of handwriting:

'The results could be taken to suggest that there is some substance in the complaint that handwriting is neglected in schools for as many as 12 per cent of the six year olds in our sample spent no time at all upon it, and among the nine year olds the figure was as high as 20 per cent.'

The Report also offered an important clue about relating handwriting to spelling:

'The child can progress to letter groups with a variety of ligatures again in common use, such as 'tion', 'ous', 'ttle', and 'ough'. Practise with these not only helps to develop speed but has the advantage of reinforcing common spelling patterns. In the course of practice children should be made aware of the rhythmical stresses of writing patterns and the affinity of letter forms which lead to a harmony of style.'

The statement that the teaching of handwriting was being neglected in schools was further endorsed by the illustrative survey, *Education 5 to 9*, written by Her Majesty's Inspectorate (1982). Here comment is made in paragraph 2.27 about the lack of systematic teaching:

'In well over half of the 5 to 8 schools regular and suitable practice of handwriting was established by the time the children reached the age of seven or eight years; fewer of the 5 to 9 schools gave the necessary attention to the development of handwriting, and only a minority arranged for systematic and regular practice and teaching.'

Overall, the report added, with the younger age groups 'some schools neglected steady practice of pattern and letter formation, and later work was adversely affected by this lack of groundwork.'

Jean Alston's (1985) report on a longitudinal study of the teaching of handwriting to pupils from first to second year junior classes in Cheshire revealed that three of the 17 county schools had staff who did not employ a consistent and comprehensive handwriting schedule and that many teachers taught handwriting only 'as the need arose'. The research also showed that, after experienced teachers had analysed inadequate performance levels in those 17 schools, 21 per cent of children were showing difficulties.

Despite the rather dismal picture painted by these comments, it is pleasing to note that there is growing interest in the teaching of handwriting in the UK. This culminated in the formation of the Handwriting Interest Group in 1983. Pressure from the group was partly responsible for the fact that the HMI document, *English from 5 to 16* (1984), was criticised for giving scant attention to the teaching of handwriting. The objective for 7-year olds simply requested that they 'write legibly', and that for 11-year olds was that they should 'exercise sufficient control over spelling, punctuation, ... syntax and handwriting to communicate their meaning effectively'. The revised document, however, gave rather more attention to handwriting by stating the following objectives for 7-year olds:

'Children should have had extensive experience of the teacher's attention and support, individually and in groups, which has included, generally and in relation to specific tasks, both diagnosis and assistance with the development of: clear handwriting, a grasp of spelling patterns, the establishment and extension of simple written sentence patterns and their elementary punctuation.'

The Kingman Report (1988), which was the result of an inquiry into the teaching of English, made only a few bland remarks about the teaching of handwriting and suggested the following attainment targets:

At 7 years
Use legible handwriting.

At 11 years
Write legibly.
Understand the different uses of cursive and printed forms of writing.

At 16 years
Write legibly and easily.
Understand the different uses of different forms of handwriting: cursive, print and capitals.

It is disturbing, however, to note that the means by which these targets are to be attained are largely ignored. The UK is now one of the few countries that have neither national guidelines nor a handwriting policy. Most Australian states and also New Zealand have, since 1984, established theirs. The United States of America, like us, has no national policy, and we are all aware of the recent concern in that country about literacy levels. Handwriting is an extremely important skill; it is essential that sound policies at both primary and secondary levels are established, if the above targets are to be realised.

2

The case for teaching joined handwriting on school entry

Although there are schools in the UK where joined writing is taught from the early years, the usual practice in most schools is to introduce young children to print script. The latter schools are concerned not so much about handwriting but about the problems that face young children learning to read. Consequently, in order to simplify these problems, they insist that children should start learning to write by copying the letter forms that they read. Reading schemes, books, cards, and classroom notices are all typeset or written in block letters and the children learn to write 'print script'. This may seem very straightforward and sensible but these schools are considering reading and not spelling.

The disadvantages of print script are as follows.

1. Print script does not follow on from the free scribble movements that children make when they first hold a pencil. These can, however, be developed into a 'running writing' style.

2. With print script, children break a natural sequence of development by learning disconnected forms and cramped movements. Later, they have another break when they have to learn 'joined up' writing. Many also revert to the disconnected letters that they first learned at school. Further on in their school career, they find themselves frustrated by being unable to put down their thoughts or take notes as quickly as they wish or need because they cannot write a cursive hand.

3. Because print script letters do not join, children do not learn how to space letters. (In cursive writing, the joining stroke makes a natural space between two letters.) One frequently sees older children's handwriting in which letters and words are written on top of each other with no intervening space at all.

4. With print script, concentration on letter formation prevents the word from flowing from the end of the pen. As adults we can sometimes produce wall charts etc. with misspellings, simply because we are concentrating on the formation of the printed letters.

Although there may be some advantages in teaching print script, these cannot possibly compensate for the above disadvantages. Instead, children should be introduced as early as possible to the making of letters through patterns. Pre-school children are doing a great deal of scribbling and they should be encouraged at this stage, and in the reception class, to discover letter shapes and movements in these scribble patterns. The shapes and movements should then be developed without a break into 'running writing'. Moreover, to wait until the age of eight before introducing a joined script is too late; at this rapidly progressing stage in their writing development, children will find a new way of handwriting too inhibiting and will consequently resist it.

The advantages of teaching joined writing are as follows.

1. It is no longer necessary to change from print to cursive in the junior years. Furthermore, the question of 'low status' does not arise, as it may do when there are children in the class who have not yet started joined writing.

2. From the beginning, words are separate. This helps children to acquire the concept of a 'word' from the very early stages of writing.

3. Correct letter formation is ensured from the beginning, since the ligatures lead into the correct starting point. Children are no longer left to 'pick up' joined writing in the junior years, with little help being given in the conventional letter formation that is crucial to legibility.

4. Spelling is helped, since letter strings are necessarily connected when writing a word.

Links with spelling

Whilst there are many handwriting schemes which must be highly recommended, the only published material that combines joined writing and spelling from the beginning is *A Hand for Spelling* (Cripps, 1988)*. Of course, it is understandable that schools may wish to continue with their existing style of writing but they should consider adapting their scheme to encourage flow and ease of joining from the beginning. It is also important that the teaching of handwriting is linked to the teaching of spelling. Good handwriting and good spelling go together and it would seem logical and more economical to teach them together. Certainly, where both skills are taught together, it is clear that children do become more confident and more aware of the structure of words, and so are able to write with speed, legibility and enthusiasm from a very early age.

Can spelling be caught?

Since the late nineteenth century, when the teaching of spelling was standard practice in schools, there have been constant rumblings about whether spelling needs to be taught at all. We know that for some children spelling is no problem; they just 'catch' it. However, there are very strong reasons why, in the cause of communication, spelling should be caught by everyone. Whilst some may consider it to be a worthwhile status symbol, its chief value lies in the freedom that it gives us to express what we want to say precisely. For example, it may be more meaningful and precise to write 'beautiful' than to resort to the over-use of 'nice'.

Before examining our spelling system, it is worth looking at factors that do not help children to catch it. Spelling is not caught merely within a stimulating linguistic experience. If it were, all linguistically favoured children would be good spellers, and we know that this is not so. Neither is spelling caught merely through listening, since the English spelling system can have more than one spelling for any one sound. For example, cup, done, does, blood, tough all contain the same sound but have different spellings. It is also possible to have more than one sound for the one spelling, for example, does, goes, shoes.

Yet, despite the evident problem of using sounds, teachers are so accustomed to equating spelling with phonics that they cannot think of the activity of spelling being other than that of sounding out a word. However, when teachers are talking about phonics, they are usually referring to phonics for reading and this is not the same as phonics for spelling. In reading, the reader is required to 'decode', that is, substitute sounds for the written symbols until the unknown word is known or 'makes sense'; in spelling, the writer is required to 'encode', that is, substitute written symbols for the meaningful sounds. Unlike reading, spelling does not make sense: there is nothing in the sounds to tell the writer that 'should' cannot be written as 'shood'. Instead, the writer must use visual memory which will be supported by

* See page 67 for further details

23

the motor skill of handwriting. Whilst the importance of phonic knowledge must be recognised, for spelling it is vital for children to be taught to LOOK at the words which they are learning and not to sound them out. For spelling, we must rely on what we SEE and not on what we HEAR.

It is also worth remembering that spelling is not 'caught' merely through reading, since we do not look at every word that we read. Indeed, there is a population of highly intelligent and literate adult readers who are poor spellers, simply because they have never needed to look at individual word structures as they read. Their poor spelling stems from the fact that they anticipated, rather than reacted to, the print. These intelligent and literate people also report that they read very fast, so that as adults they still do not look at the internal structure of words.

What is our spelling system like?

If we know what spelling is like, if we can describe our model of spelling, we can then appreciate the extent to which catching can be facilitated in the early years.

Peters (1985) argues that our spelling system is not unsystematic and unpredictable, but instead, it is based on the probability of letters occurring together, that is, letters that stick together. She cites the work of Gibson and Levin (1975) who said that 'spelling is a kind of grammar for letter sequences that generates permissible combinations without regard to sound'. Peters describes this as 'a scale of probability, ranging from letters that *can* occur in sequence to those that *cannot* occur, that is, from highly probable to highly improbable even impossible letter sequences'. It is not a matter of whether a word is regular or irregular. Words that cannot be decoded, that is, grapho-phonemically regular, are still made up in a sequentially probable manner. Such a sequence *can* happen; we know that it can happen because the letters 'look right'. We do this when we do not know how to spell a word, since we 'write it down to see if it looks right'. Sight is our preferred sense, and this is a reliable check to spelling. However, the visual appearance is not as important as the knowledge of letter by letter structure or what we call letter patterns or letter strings.

Adults are aware of serial probability as a result of doing crosswords or else simply by being intrigued by word structure. If this is so, then they will notice likenesses within words and be in a position to recognise letter strings. This is where the teacher is able to promote the catching of spelling. Children who have 'caught' spelling are familiar with letter sequences in the world around them. The teacher can direct children's attention to looking at words within words or at interesting letter patterns or letter strings that are 'in my name' or are like the name of a sweet or a detergent or other product that appears in the child's vicinity. Children must also be taught to make visual associations between words, that is, be taught groups of words which look the same irrespective of their sound. During any discussion about the 'look' of a word, the letter names must be used and not the sounds of the letters.

We do not 'look with intent' unless we have a reason for doing so. In the case of spelling, this is to reproduce a word. The teacher must encourage the children to look closely at the word before writing it, must point out the interesting features, and must challenge the children to be able to reproduce the word without copying.

When talking about spelling, teachers will probably be thinking about 'words'. The strategy of writing from memory, however, must be encouraged from the very beginning, that is, from the early stages of handwriting patterns, single letters, and letter strings. This early practice of writing from memory will help the children to meet the challenge of writing whole words because they will already have rehearsed the letters and letter strings contained in the whole word. *A Hand for Spelling* (Cripps, 1988) provides numerous activities to facilitate the teaching of this technique from the beginning.

Is there a reliable strategy for learning to spell?

Probably the most important skill to teach children is to write from memory. Whenever children are learning new words it is essential that they keep to the following routine:

LOOK   at the word carefully and in such a way that it will be remembered.

COVER the word so that it cannot be seen.

WRITE   the word from memory.

CHECK what has been written. If the word has not been written correctly, do not alter it but, instead, repeat all these steps again.

Teachers should be careful that 'Look, Cover, Write, Check' does not become a mere 'catch phrase' which results in children simply copying the word, letter by letter. Instead, the children must be challenged to remember the whole word and to write it from memory. It is here that handwriting is so important, because 'speed of writing is clearly basic to spelling progress' (Peters, 1985) and speed of writing is determined by legibility and letter formation. Surely this is best acquired through the most economic and effective movement, that is, through the practising of letter strings (for example, *ter*, *ame*, *ood*) in joined writing. In other words, by combining the secretarial skills of handwriting and spelling at this early stage, children will be free to concentrate on the compositional aspects of writing.

Will children become so concerned about handwriting and spelling that the essential creative element will be lost?

Children must be given confidence, otherwise they may become so concerned about handwriting and spelling that the essential creative element in writing will be lost. Sadly, a child's perception of writing often relates very strongly to the neatness of writing and the correctness of spelling. The research by Bennett et al. (1985), in observing 16 able teachers of top infant children, produced evidence that teachers were overstressing handwriting when asking children to write creatively. It was found that, in 70 per cent of the 13 tasks that were aimed at the development of writing skills, teachers conformed to a regular pattern of exposition and questioning, followed by emphasis on neatness of writing, whenever the children started to commit thoughts to paper. The research team also found that interchanges between pupils and teacher were dominated by the request for spellings. These findings were further confirmed by the pupils, who were clear that neatness was one of the important criteria that the teacher would use in marking. The concern of many people must be that extra emphasis on handwriting at 5 years old would only exacerbate the overdominance of secretarial skills that are demanded by teachers.

Hall (1987), in an article evaluating what young children understood about the printed word, implored teachers to allow young children to engage in literate behaviours from a very early stage. He extolled the virtues of scribble writing and of giving the children a chance to experiment in the written form, thus discovering the pleasure of communicating through writing. Hall concluded his article by saying, 'How tragic it is when, all too frequently, children are exposed to sterile, pointless, meaningless and futile sets of exercises involving nothing more dynamic than copying.' Discerning teachers always wish to maintain excitement in the writing process for children and they aim to educate the children to become people who have many writing skills. How, then, do they balance the great emphasis on handwriting skill at 5 years old with the need to promote a breadth of communication skills?

Clay (1975) summarises her view, that the handwriting process inhibits the writing process, when she states:

> 'When a young child attempts to write a story the mechanical aspects of the task create a very long delay between the first letter and the last full stop. In the tedious labour of formulating new words in print the child often loses the meaning or the grammatical structure he began with.'

It seems, therefore, that there are two issues to consider:

1   The need to provide children with the essential secretarial skills for writing.

2   The need for teachers and children not to develop the habit of believing that, when composing a written piece of work, the most significant part of the work is the handwriting and spelling.

Handwriting serves writing. The prime functional importance of handwriting is to convey, legibly, the writer's message to the reader. As such, it is important that this purely physical skill is taught correctly from the outset. Nevertheless, one of the major reasons for teaching joined handwriting from the beginning is to enable children by the age of 7 years, just when the desire to write is reaching its fullest momentum, to have mastery over this particular skill. So often, in the normal approach to the teaching of handwriting, children are inhibited by the requirement to cast off their successful printing and to start to learn a joined writing.

In schools where joined writing is taught to children on school entry, the overwhelming comment has been that the 6-7 year old children exhibit confidence and competency in both handwriting and spelling skills. Comments such as 'a significant increase in independence', ... 'much more aware of words', ... 'those children who started out on joined writing are the most confident in handwriting and spelling', ... 'my children are happy at writing', ... 'children are aware of the structure of words' indicate a healthy situation in these classrooms.

The emphasis that teachers place on handwriting and spelling skills must also be given consideration. The most crucial balance is that between handwriting lessons themselves and the development in young children of the concept that handwriting conveys a message. Clay comments: 'Observation of children suggests that they do not learn about language on any one level of organisation before they manipulate units at higher levels.' This intermingling of the learning of letters, words, and finally word groups is certainly not hierarchical. During the process, children must be given the opportunity to use handwriting as a tool for that learning. It is only allowing children to over-experiment with their handwriting development that could lead to irretrievable mistakes.

Surely these two aspects can co-exist in the classroom. Far from inhibiting creative writing, the strong emphasis in the early years on word inspection and on discussion about words and their structure is part and parcel of any approach that increases children's confidence and pleasure in writing.

3

Practical implications for teaching joined handwriting and spelling

Whenever any curriculum innovation is proposed which involves the whole school, it is important to consider the implications very carefully. Such an innovation must not be rushed. At the outset, perceived difficulties must be highlighted; research, or authoritative comment, should be considered in order to ensure success. For each perceived problem there are likely to be some practical implications which would effect a change in either the teaching approach or the organisation of the classroom. By drawing on comments from a wide range of teachers, this chapter addresses itself to the practical implications of introducing joined handwriting on school entry. Discussion will focus on issues relating to the children's learning and to teachers and parents.

Issues relating to the children

Will children be able to read joined writing?

In talking to teachers about the principle of teaching joined writing to 5 and 6-year olds, this is one of the most regularly expressed concerns. To some extent, the research from Indiana that is quoted by Early (1976) allays the suspicion by indicating that the delay in teaching joined writing may have depended on tradition rather than on any scientific evidence. If we were to find that reading a joined script presented problems, it would be safe to assume that the idea of teaching joined writing would founder. There is a widespread feeling among teachers that children do find it difficult to read joined writing but this is probably based on two misapprehensions: first, that children even as old as 7 or 8 years often state that they cannot read joined script, and secondly, that 5-year olds would be too young to read joined script. With persuasion, the 7 and 8-year olds have little difficulty as long as the presented model is clear. In schools where joined writing is taught from the beginning, the following comment is often voiced in staffrooms: 'I believe that we have been underestimating these children all the time.'

In one school, the reception class teacher, who uses the *Breakthrough to Literacy* material to teach reading, had in the third week of term a group of children who could recognise approximately 15 words. She presented these same words on identical cards in joined writing. The children were asked to match both sets of words and, without further explanation, were able to pick out the pairs. On further questioning they confidently told the teacher that the words 'said the same'.

In another school, where children were taught only to print, Michael (5.3 years) and Elaine (5.4 years), who had both started to read with confidence, were presented with the following sentence in joined writing: 'My mummy is sitting in the garden.' Both children were asked if they noticed anything different in the writing. They both stated that it was 'double writing'. Michael then explained further that, in double writing, 'it keeps going'. They were then asked to point to some words and it was obvious from their reaction that they had a concept of a word. The most significant factor was that both of these children were able to read the sentence independently. They then enjoyed further success with the following sentence: 'I am going to school to do some painting with my teacher.' Not only did they both read the sentence but they were also predicting each word after the first few letters were written. It was obvious that these two children were not inhibited by being exposed to joined writing. Teachers may like to try this activity in their own schools.

It seems that the only practical implication of this procedure is that children should have the chance to read both print and joined writing. A sensible level of discussion with children who are beginning to read will support the need to spot the differences and to talk about letters, joins, and whole words. Schools may use a variety of approaches to provide children with an environment in which there is joined writing to read. For example, a school might take the extreme step of ensuring that all reading material provided by the teacher (wall displays, home-made books, word books, etc.) is presented to the children in the school's handwriting style. Most schools, however, would probably take the view that any teacher-produced reading material for reading should be *printed* and any displays or words for writing should be *written* in the school's handwriting style. It would not be uncommon to see some words which are used for reading and writing in both printed and cursive form.

From experience and observation it is quite clear that, if the letters are well formed, children are able to read joined writing. It is for the school to decide whether to opt for 'total submersion' or for a mixture of print and joined writing.

What kind of perceptual activities will help children to differentiate between letters and joins?

In order to help children to recognise the difference between letters and joins, the teacher must provide games and activities that will promote perceptual awareness. In addition, the children must be constantly involved in a great deal of discussion about the shape of letters and the ways in which they are joined together.

Jigsaws, looking at patterns, using matching materials, and spot-the-difference games all help to increase the children's visual acuity. Pattern making, using a variety of art and craft media (see P. 49), gives a rich variety of experience in order for children to develop an understanding of the perceptual form of a letter. At this stage oral work relating to the physical shaping of the letters will assist the children in 'seeing' the whole letter. For example, in teaching the letter 'g', the teacher might say: 'Start at the dot and come back round and up to the dot; now straight down and curl round to make a swing for someone to sit in.'

In one particular school, a teacher was heard to give the group of letters a,c,d,g,o,q the generic title of the 'one o'clock club'. All of the children knew that, as a result of talking about how to write this group of letters, the writing implement had to be taken to the one o'clock position before starting the letter. This reinforcement of the letter shape by talking through the physical action helps to confirm perception in children's minds. The learning of joins, or ligatures, is an important stage in the development of joined writing. If the separate letter is already well established, the join often follows quite naturally.

Five-year old children are quite capable of coping with letters and joins as long as the separate nature of each letter is taught first. In one school, reception-aged children were asked to count or point to the letters and joins in a prepared piece of joined writing. Without any hesitation they were able to identify letters or joins. Many of the children were also able to state that a word had more letters than joins. This activity is to be recommended. Writing from memory must also be promoted throughout all writing activities.

Do 5-year olds have the motor control for joining letters?

Although there is a strong link with the previous question regarding children's perceptual abilities, it is worth considering separately whether the process of actually joining letters is a development of fine motor control that is too mature for a 5-year old child. Certainly Sassoon (1983) warns us that 'to push children into trying to form letters before their hand and eye co-ordination, and their ability to perceive or copy, are sufficiently developed, causes tension and probably problems later on' However, she does add that, whilst 'joining up letters needs maturity of thinking as well as co-ordination', children's abilities are often underestimated. She continues by indicating that 'if it is taught properly from the start, handwriting need not be difficult' and that 'exercises work quickly on five year olds'. Her philosophy is most supportive of the notion of teaching joined writing to young children when she states that one of her major priorities for a handwriting model is a 'flowing first alphabet that leads naturally into cursive'. Separate letters with joining strokes are quite within the capabilities of 5-year olds.

Jarman (1979) expresses some concern about a completely joined hand as a first introduction to writing but he does say:

> 'Printing is almost the *opposite* of writing. It is laborious and unjoined and is not done with handwriting movements. Many infants who learn to print script develop serious problems in handwriting for the rest of their school days..... Many teachers in the past have given their children rhythmic handwriting patterns and taught them to print script. But these are essentially two completely opposed activities.'

Although it is plain from the examples quoted earlier that young readers are able to notice the difference in print and cursive styles, it is crucial to develop in the children a pattern awareness in preparation for writing. The increased perceptual awareness that is needed for coping with joined writing is obvious: not only do letters have to be formed but the linking strokes must also complete the total pattern made by the word. As a part of their writing readiness, children are going to have to progress through the stages of being aware of patterns all around them, of being able to make their own patterns, and finally of seeing the relationship between letters and patterns. Having achieved this perceptual stage, the final step is to develop the necessary hand/eye co-ordination and fine motor control.

Consequently, children must spend more time in looking at patterns in an increasingly refined way until they closely match those of joined letter formation. With this change of approach, children could be delayed beyond the current expectation time for recording with a pencil. Children should not be asked to record with a pencil and paper too early, that is, before letter formation has been firmly established. Obviously many children will have 'learned' to write before school entry and it would be very unwise to inhibit any desire to communicate or to produce inventive writing in any way; children must always be encouraged to enjoy 'writing'. Moreover, parents will undoubtedly be asking to see the writing done by their children. The point is not to force children into the blind copying of letters or words, which have yet to be taught.

If children are asked to record thoughts in writing before the skill of letter formation is learned, many incorrect habits are created which are extremely difficult to remedy. Also, the excitement of recording is often destroyed by too much writing in the early years. Instead, make use of alternative ways of recording, such as the following.

1. *Breakthrough to Literacy*: The children make their own sentences using either the teacher's or their own sentence maker and stand. These sentences may be read to someone at the same time, left out for others to read, recorded in their own book or the

class book by the teacher who uses either print or a joined script, typed using a jumbo typewriter, or fed into a word processor.

The following example shows how one child has used the classroom resource of prepared words by pasting her story onto paper before drawing a picture (see Fig. 13). By doing this, Michelle, in her first term of school, is not being told to 'copy' letters she has yet to be taught.

Figure 13
Michelle (5.3 years)

2. Concept Keyboard (a simple touch sensitive keyboard used with a microcomputer): An ideal method of producing a sentence using common words and then printing them ready for making into a book.

3. Using a typist: Children gain immense satisfaction out of dictating a story to a person who is proficient on the keyboard.

4. Drawing a series of 'comic' sketches: These pictures may relate a story, a visit, or some other happening and the 'author' can then tell the story of the pictures.

5. Using a tape recorder: Children can soon become proficient at using a tape recorder. By careful use of the pause button, a good story can be developed for other people, especially parents at home.

Since the need to develop the pattern concept means delaying the introduction to writing letters, for up to a whole term in the case of children with poor perception and motor control, it is necessary to provide children with opportunities to practise pattern work. Probably the best way to increase children's patterning ability as well as motor control is through art and craft.

Mention must also be made here of the need to ensure that some of the pattern work is done by the children on the vertical plane rather than solely on the horizontal. One of the objectives behind these patterns is to train the children into flowing movements preparatory for writing, which of course is to be done on a desk top. Having created the patterns in a large dimension, the children will reach a stage where the patterns can be drawn using a pencil or felt-tip pen. As a general rule the patterns should have some similarity to the shapes of letters.

Marion Richardson (1935) said that 'rhythmic pattern movements make it possible for the child to experience the essentially cursive nature of handwriting from the beginning, even before he has learned to write.'

Jarman (1979) argued that 'the first writing movements should be those handwriting movements which we wish the child to retain for a life time.' It is also important that pattern work continues throughout the children's development towards a mature hand and is not seen simply as a stage in the continuum which is to be forgotten once mastered.

Much of what has been said about pattern and pencil control emphasises the need to retain a flowing action without lifting the writing implement from the paper. By the time that children are ready to begin forming letters, they will have a loose wrist, comfortable control of the pencil, good perception, and well-developed fine motor control. Consequently the flowing separate letter must be taught as an immediate preparation for joining. The flowing separate letter, in the view of Sassoon (1983), is quite within the capability of a 5-year old and, if it is correctly formed, leads naturally into cursive.

This is all very different from the traditional ball-and-stick print; that approach to writing encourages children to produce letters by drawing the round part and then adding the stick, usually causing a pen lift of some sort. For example, the letter 'a' would be formed by producing a 'c' shape and then adding the stick from the top of the letter. Likewise, a 'd' would be formed by producing the same 'c' shape and adding the stick from the top down. The letters a, b, g, d, p, q are most likely to produce this very staccato approach to letter formation.

The flowing letter, however, is formed in such a way that in the majority of letters the pencil is not lifted whilst writing a letter and finishes in a position where logical joining strokes may follow naturally at a later stage in development.

It must be emphasised that the correct formation of the letter is essential before considering the question of joins, or ligatures. Decisions must be made regarding which letters to join and then the ligatures should be taught and practised until they become automatic. It is not necessary to wait until all letters have been taught; join two or three letter strings as part of the handwriting practice, for example, 'ca', 'en', 'at'. As these letter strings are also part of our spelling system, the links with spelling are made. *A Hand for Spelling* will provide teachers with classroom material which is based on words that children use in their writing. As the children progress and gain competence in all letters, the complete set of ligatures are taught using the teaching principles mentioned elsewhere.

Moreover, mastery of letter formation and natural joins encourages children to enjoy writing. One of the first words that most children want to write is their own name, often in simple sentences. Make full use of each child's name and use it to extend the writing of other words. For example, Jason could write his name and the smaller words within it (see Fig. 14).

Figure 14
Jason (5.6 years old)

There is no doubt that young children are able to cope with joining letters provided that they achieve the correct development of fine motor control through the use of art and craft media, a progression of pattern work, and the teaching of letters that lead naturally to a cursive style. However, it should always be remembered that the learning process is a continuum and that the development of children will be inhibited if they are forced at any time into a stage beyond their capabilities.

Will children be confused when copying from a printed form?

Much of the children's reading environment is in the printed form, for example, commercial word charts, dictionaries, and of course the wealth of reading books that is available in schools. As children start to write, they will use these materials as resources for words. Will confusion set in as they see the print image and try to write it in a joined style? Is it really practical to convert all printed material which is being used in this way into a joined style? If children are unable to use these resources then the idea of teaching joined writing from the outset is surely unwise.

Little has been written about this issue beyond Edward Johnston's main argument in 1913 in favour of the change from a copperplate to a printed style. His case rested on the fact that, since children's reading material is in the printed form, it would help both the writing and reading processes if a printed format were also used.

On the other hand, if the formation of letters is well taught then the children should not have any particular difficulty in seeing a printed word and writing it out in a cursive style. The question of labels on wall displays and so on will undoubtedly be of concern to some teachers. Interestingly, children do not experience any difficulty when converting print to joined writing (see Fig. 15). What is important is that the teacher must present a joined style when writing in the children's books. Occasionally, some children may produce a printed letter in their writing. This should not be viewed as a problem because the letter may be in a strange or unusual cluster of letters or it may be the first letter of the child's name which will have been rehearsed many times in another context. If the difference is pointed out, the teacher will find that in a very short time the children will be writing the word in a complete joined style.

Will children who move either from or into a school that teaches joined writing suffer setbacks?

The problem of pupil mobility should be considered by all schools involved in a curriculum initiative, as it would be educationally unacceptable if children were to suffer an unnecessary setback on changing schools. It is widely recognised that a move to another school presents traumas of many kinds for children. The additional issue of whether the teaching of joined writing at this stage would cause confusion either for children moving away from the school or for children entering from a printing environment cannot be overlooked.

Figure 15
Example of a 5- year old converting print to joined writing
Taken from a printed poem

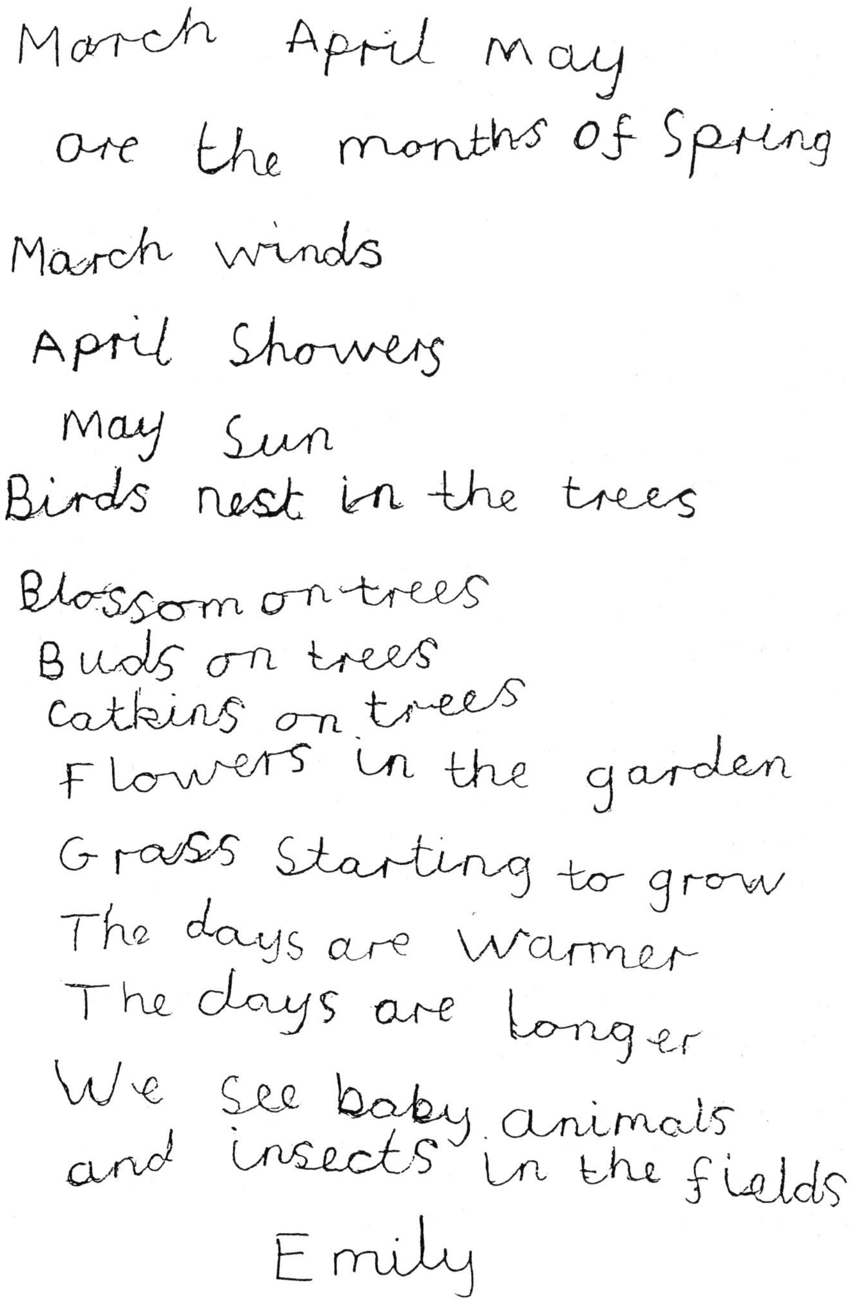

March April May
are the months of Spring

March winds

April Showers

May Sun
Birds nest in the trees

Blossom on trees
Buds on trees
Catkins on trees
Flowers in the garden

Grass Starting to grow
The days are warmer
The days are longer
We See baby animals
and insects in the fields
Emily

Generally, children leaving a school which does joined writing should not suffer any particular setback for the following reasons.

1. All of the pre-writing patterns and fine motor control activities are conducive to good letter formation. Increased concentration on this aspect would benefit whichever approach to writing is used.

2. At the stage of teaching flowing letters, there is little difference between those letters and the usual print letters which are required by other teachers. The former have the major advantage of being composed in a continuous flow with no lift of the writing implement from the paper.

3. Once children have started to join letters, there would be two options open to the receiving teacher: to allow the children to continue to develop a joined style or, if the school insisted on print script, to allow the children to transfer to the required approach by using the flowing separate letters. It is hoped that the exit ligatures of these letters would be accepted even though they might look untidy to the teacher requiring a neat and concise letter.

The problem of children moving into a system which is employing a joined writing approach also needs consideration. Must the children be stopped from writing whilst the new approach is learned or should they be told to continue working through the exercise whilst writing print? Would a gradual process of assimilation be possible? Here again it will be found that the children cope surprisingly easily with not only the concept of joined writing but also the physical movement required for the joins. There will, of course, be a transition stage when some children learn certain letter joins more easily than others. Obviously, the teacher must observe the children's writing very closely, must look for any incorrect letter formation and, by studying the finished product, must highlight the letters that are not joined. The biggest problem is posed by those children who have learned incorrect letter formation and who find difficulty in producing a proper flow from letter to letter. In other words, introducing joined writing at middle and top infant stages is hardest when a child has poor handwriting skills. This is also one of the key factors in the changeover at a later stage. If there is a deficiency in skill then surely the sooner it is tackled the better. Otherwise, the faults may be so heavily ingrained by the age of eight that remediation becomes a major physical and emotional task.

Teachers should always be prepared for any emotional strain which is posed by this situation and should spend time defusing the problem with new entrants. Children will accept the new writing style and are soon able to pick up simple joins. The teacher can then help with any of the ligatures or letters that they find difficult.

The awareness that other children are writing in a more 'grown-up' fashion than they themselves can also inspire children to write in a similar way. Moreover, children adapt to joining from a print style more easily in the early stages than later on. In those few cases where children feel 'different' on entering a school where print script is definitely not for infants or where they (and parents) may gain the impression of never being able to match the standards, sympathetic teaching should overcome the difficulties with ease.

Issues relating to the teacher

There is little doubt that any curriculum change in a school needs careful planning and thought. A significant part of that thinking is concerned with how teachers will assimilate the change into their understanding of the issue at hand and how they will have to alter their present mode of working. This is achieved by regular discussion within the staffroom, ironing out problems as they occur and planning strategies to overcome them.

This section considers the difficulties which may occur and outlines some of the solutions, in both philosophical and practical terms, so that new members of staff may receive a well-structured and meaningful induction programme.

What is the theory behind the principle?

This interesting question should not be overlooked. For example, in one school, a recently appointed teacher who was taking the reception class reported how much support she had received from her colleagues regarding classroom organisation, pre-writing ideas, and the teaching of letter shapes. She indicated that she was coming to terms with the changes from her previous school but then asked, 'Why are we teaching joined writing at such an early stage?' It seems that, with all the other pressures involved in settling into a new school, this vital factor had not been mentioned. By being concerned only with the practicalities of teaching, there is a danger of excluding new teachers from the opportunity of understanding the rationale behind the whole concept. It is important, therefore, that there is reading material available and also a chance for discussion with an involved teacher.

What level of writing should be expected from each age group?

Teachers must always rely on a well-developed pedagogic understanding of all that they teach since, without this, they cannot be effective in providing the correct teaching at the right time for any group of children. Teaching is not effective if the teacher is only one step ahead. It is also true that children's learning does not always follow an exact linear progression and consequently a teacher needs a complete overview of the learning process. The following guide may help teachers to understand this process. Of course, the progression shown might not be totally adhered to by all children but it could at least be a checklist for teaching. The omission of age levels is intentional; there is such a wide spectrum of ability and experience that rigidly following any age-related steps would have its dangers. Finally, no one idea can be dealt with, learned, and then forgotten. Many of the areas mentioned *must* be repeated in a variety of ways throughout children's writing development.

A GUIDE FOR DEVELOPING CHILDREN'S WRITING

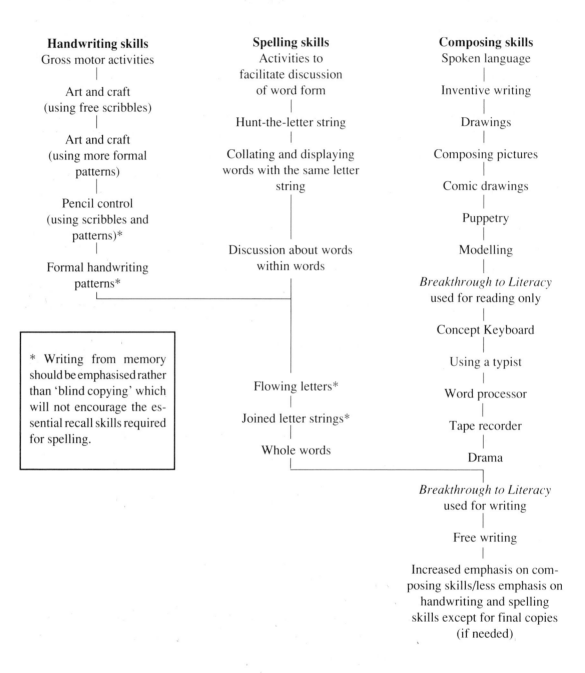

Handwriting skills

Gross motor activities

|

Art and craft
(using free scribbles)

|

Art and craft
(using more formal
patterns)

|

Pencil control
(using scribbles and
patterns)*

|

Formal handwriting
patterns*

---

* Writing from memory should be emphasised rather than 'blind copying' which will not encourage the essential recall skills required for spelling.

Spelling skills

Activities to
facilitate discussion
of word form

|

Hunt-the-letter string

|

Collating and displaying
words with the same letter
string

Discussion about words
within words

Flowing letters*

|

Joined letter strings*

|

Whole words

Composing skills

Spoken language

|

Inventive writing

|

Drawings

|

Composing pictures

|

Comic drawings

|

Puppetry

|

Modelling

|

Breakthrough to Literacy
used for reading only

Concept Keyboard

|

Using a typist

|

Word processor

|

Tape recorder

|

Drama

Breakthrough to Literacy
used for writing

|

Free writing

|

Increased emphasis on composing skills/less emphasis on handwriting and spelling skills except for final copies
(if needed)

The guide separates the three aspects of development from the start because both spelling and composing skills are all too often inhibited by premature use of a writing implement. It is vital that the children are given a full chance to develop their observational and oral skills, which are essential to spelling, long before they are asked to write letters. A wide spectrum of activities related to word inspection, collections of single letters and of groups, and other perceptual tasks must be experienced before the skills of writing letters are introduced. This mirrors the need for developing good pre-writing skills, as already mentioned on P.31.

As handwriting and spelling skills develop, they must be linked together. This is the vital stage when writing from memory must be encouraged. Once children have learned the correct motor action that is involved in forming a flowing separate letter, it is essential to encourage activities that develop automatic recall of that action rather than direct copying. This concept must then be enlarged by the joining of two- and three-letter strings and by the teaching of whole words. The teacher must always remember this sequence: first, teach the motor action and consolidate it; second, encourage close inspection for similarities and differences; third, emphasise writing from memory. With confidence and freedom developing alongside the children's ability to write words, the time is appropriate to combine these handwriting and spelling skills with the children's creative thoughts. At this stage the essential secretarial skills should be developing strongly enough to be supportive rather than restrictive.

It was mentioned above that no particular age should be attributed to various stages. However, from experience the approximate ages for each level of development might be as follows.

4.5 - 5.0 years	Pre-writing patterns.
5.0 - 5.5 years	Separate flowing letters.
5.5 - 6.0 years	Beginning to join letters in words and writing own name.
6.0 - 6.5 years	Joining all letters in words.
6.5 - 7.5 years	Producing joined writing with confidence.
7.5 years onwards	Developing a personalised hand if the basic formation of letters and joins is correct.
8.0 years onwards	Learning how to print for diagrams, labels, etc.

It cannot be overemphasised that this is only a suggested, 'rule of thumb' progression and that there is tremendous danger in asking too much of children too soon. There are some children who come to school with very little motor control or awareness of words and who, throughout their school life, will receive little outside support. They must, of course, be encouraged to achieve at their fullest potential but introducing any of the stages too early could cause irreparable damage.

Conversely, the ability of young children to learn joined writing must not be underestimated. One teacher who had been teaching 10-year olds in another school and was now with a class of top infants remarked: 'I am stunned by the quality of handwriting and confidence in spelling shown by the 7-year olds in my new class. They are, overall, vastly superior to the 10-year olds in my previous class.'

If this approach is adopted, must the school change its current handwriting model?

The answer is dependent on whether the style is cursive and whether there is a consistent approach throughout the school. If the current style is one in which the exit ligatures which are taken from the bottom of letters are straight and create an angular look, this sharp 'ticking' approach would create a jerky flow in writing and so the style might need to change in order for the joins to be made with ease.

If the style is italic, much more consideration will need to be given to the flowing nature of the joins.

Throughout the handwriting programme, there will be a general move towards developing a personal hand. This can be achieved only if the children have had a solid foundation on which to experiment and develop their own short-cuts and idiosyncrasies. It is strongly suggested, therefore, that the school's taught style should be adhered to for a good period of time in order to ensure a secure basic hand.

As stated previously, it is important for lower juniors to be given a static print model which can be used when labelling diagrams, maps, etc. This is a useful skill and a short session of practice, coupled with the opportunity to use print, is essential.

Must a teacher's own print script style be changed to a joined style?

The answer to this question is clearly yes and will certainly be a problem facing many teachers. They will need to spend time practising the decided style of the school. Staff meetings and regular discussion will help teachers to make the necessary changes. Generally, after a term most teachers will be confident with their own writing.

Will classroom organisation have to change?

The Bullock Report (1975) stated quite clearly that:

> 'If a child is left to develop his handwriting without instruction he is unlikely to develop a running hand which is simultaneously legible, fast-flowing, and individual and becomes effortless to produce. We therefore believe that the teacher should devote time to teaching it and to giving the children ample practice.'

This simple statement means that teachers will be required to give very careful consideration to classroom management, organisation of furniture, the pupils' time, their own time, and the use of other adults.

Sassoon (1983) supports the theory that handwriting is a necessary skill that needs time:

> 'In today's crowded classrooms there must be sympathy for the overworked teacher with pressure for visible progress of all sorts. ... However, priorities must be established within the curriculum. Skill writing lessons are needed from the start, separate from and complementary to creative writing. What really worries me, after several years of specific research into handwriting problems in schools, is the indifference of so many teachers to these very problems. They see no importance in skill training and the damage they are doing to young children is not evident until several years later.'

From this statement and those made in the illustrative survey by HMI in 1982, it is clear that within UK schools too little thought is being given to the teaching of handwriting. Many teachers have been left to develop their own approach to letter formation. This often results in their rejecting an attempt to teach a running hand at the age of eight. However, in accepting the theory, teachers must consider very carefully how they will modify their daily classroom organisation in order to cater for the teaching of handwriting without inhibiting the children's natural desire to record thoughts on paper. They must take account of the following aspects: group teaching, seating arrangements, the time allotted, and the use of other adults.

In recent years, direct teaching to a group of infant children has fallen out of favour, particularly with regard to the teaching of handwriting. Now when the need for group teaching is mentioned to teachers there are raised eyebrows with mixed comments such as: 'Surely that is not what is expected these days?' or 'Thank goodness, does that mean the fashion is changing back?' There is no doubt that in the teaching of a physical skill such as handwriting the teacher must be able to observe directly each child's posture, grip of the implement, and movement. Demonstration by the teacher, either to a group or an individual, is as important as observation. Coupled with this is the advantage gained by the children when talking about the words, the letters, and the movement required to write them.

Generally, it has been found that group sizes of 6 to 10 children are the optimum for reception and middle infants, with perhaps slightly larger groups for older children. The advantage of not teaching the whole class is obvious: the range of ability is often very wide, especially at the crucial age of 5-6 years. Teachers must also consider very carefully these differing abilities when selecting the group members. The only time that a whole class of children could be practising handwriting is at the end of the infant stage, when the essential teaching of letter formation is superseded by the need for regular practice.

Seating arrangements also need careful thought. The vast majority of infant classes arrange seating around groups of tables. If the handwriting groups are working on individual tasks then this seating is satisfactory. However, when the instruction uses a chalk-and-talk approach, it is recommended that all of the children are seated facing the chalkboard. This arrangement has several advantages:

1. When a physical action is demonstrated by the teacher, all of the children see the same movement.

2. The teacher, when watching children tracing in the air, can more easily identify incorrect movements.

3. All of the children are facing the chalkboard and so there is no looking over the shoulder.

This change of teaching style will also necessitate a change in time allocation. Although many teachers say that they teach handwriting, a great deal of the work is done by the children working unobserved by the teacher. In many instances, the handwriting is judged only by the finished product, much of which may look 'neat' but which contains many letters that have been formed incorrectly. This can be avoided if the children are observed continually in the early stages of learning to write.

In one week a class of reception/middle infant children should be exposed to a variety of handwriting experiences within the following timetable:

1. One 20-30 minute session as a large group, when the relevant language work and general discussion takes place.

2. Three or four sessions of up to 30 minutes with small groups for related activities according to the stage of the children. These groups may be determined by motor control. Remember that the small-group and individual sessions may be supervised by an informed ancillary helper.

3. Individual children will require specific help and programmes.

Although this may seem excessive, if it is linked with the skill of spelling as well as with art and craft, it is really a very small portion of the week's timetable. Obviously, the amount of time will vary in differing circumstances but the most important issue is that time is spent teaching this vital skill.

Finally, consideration must be given as to how adult helpers may be used in the teaching. It is strongly advised that parents are encouraged to be involved in the classroom and in the teaching of handwriting. This has two advantages: it informs many of the children's parents about the process and it allows the important direct observation to continue while the teacher is perhaps helping an individual child. Parents will, of course, require advice and this can best be achieved through in-service by either direct teaching or observation of the teacher with children. Parents must be clear about the objectives for each session and should never be given continuous responsibility for a group. If care is taken in the planning then this shared responsibility can only be of benefit to the children.

Will parents and pre-school leaders resist the change and be confused when helping their children?

It is essential to consider any predicted problem in this area because the support of parents and pre-school leaders is central to the success of such an innovation. It may, therefore, take a number of meetings to explain the rationale behind such a curriculum change. However, it would be very unusual for parents to show a lack of enthusiasm and support, since it seems to them that their children will be learning something earlier than usual, which is always a positive feeling. More importantly, the idea makes sense. Some parents may be concerned about the problem facing their children if they move school (see p.36 for a response to this concern).

Both parents and pre-school leaders should be fully informed of the teaching progression that is involved, especially in the pre-writing stage, and they should be encouraged to avoid teaching pre-school children to print, especially in capital letters.

4

Resources and teaching techniques

This chapter addresses itself to the practicalities of classroom management by offering a wide variety of ideas which will help children to learn to write legibly with speed, confidence and enthusiasm. These ideas are based on the premise that the natural flowing scribble of young children should be harnessed into pattern work from which a 'running hand' will follow. The ideas also link spelling with handwriting in order that the two skills can be learned together.

In any handwriting programme, the first priority should be legibility. If handwriting is the means of communication then it must be easy to read with the letters properly formed. At a later stage, children will require different levels of writing for different purposes: very fast for personal notes, clear but quick for general use, and a formal hand for special occasions.

The second priority is speed. This is particularly important as the children become older and enter the secondary school where they are expected to do a great deal of note-taking. In most cases the fast printer is not as fast as the person who uses a cursive style.

Finally, children must be encouraged to develop a personal hand by breaking away from the taught model. This will only be successful if the foundations are secure. This personal hand usually begins when joined writing is established and indicates the writer's confidence and maturity.

Ideas for developing motor control and hand/eye co-ordination

These activities should be readily available in the reception class and to any other child who needs to develop motor control. Many of the ideas are variations on a common theme and should not be seen as sequential. Moreover, there are many events which occur naturally throughout the day and which may be utilised, for example, tying knots and bows, buttoning, zipping coats, or screwing lids on jars.

Ball games

Rolling, bowling, throwing and catching large balls and, later, smaller balls.

Tearing, cutting and folding paper

Tearing paper is a suitable activity for young children whereas using scissors is more suited to older children.

Cutting and pasting

Cutting and tearing pictures from magazines to paste and construct mosaics.

Construction

Blocks, Lego and Unifix materials, and construction toys which utilise hammering will all assist muscular as well as hand/eye co-ordination.

Jigsaw puzzles

Simple jigsaws with very few large pieces to complex puzzles with many small pieces can be provided according to the children's ability.

Toys and games

Toys requiring finger manipulation, such as typewriters, computer games, cash registers, and bead threading encourage the development of fine motor co-ordination, the integration of hand/eye movement, and the establishment of hand preference.

Finger rhymes

There are many finger rhymes in which children can participate, such as: 'Incy Wincy Spider', 'Where Is Thumbkin?' and 'My Hands Are Shaking'. All help to establish finger control.

Finger play

With the thumb, children touch each of the fingers in order. Later, they can try touching thumb to fingers, using both hands at once. Older children can try this exercise with the eyes closed.

Pattern work through art and craft

Most children should have had the chance to experience making and seeing pattern work in the form of art and craft before proceeding into fine pencil control work. Do not presume that they have the required experience before applying the fine control that is needed in pencil work. The following suggestions should provide teachers with ideas for classroom activities. These range from the early motor skills to the kind of pattern work that is necessary for pre-writing skills.

Moulding

Various shapes can be moulded by using clay, sand, play dough, baking dough, putty, sawdust, oatmeal, papier mâché, etc.

Clay or Plasticine

By using clay or Plasticine, each child can roll out a fairly long and thin sausage - a skill in itself - and then place it along patterns that are drawn on laminated card. The teacher must always ensure that the children work from the left to the right of the card as well as from the top to the bottom. Having completed their card, children could be encouraged to take a rubbing of the result.

Another idea entails rolling out a flat piece of Plasticine and then etching a pattern on it.

Finger painting

Many schools have special finger paints to encourage children to paint without brushes. This concept is easily transferred to the pattern-making ideas. Initially, children should be encouraged to use either hand to allow a hand preference to be determined. When hand dominance has been determined, emphasis may be placed on the use of the 'writing finger', that is, the pointing finger on the natural writing hand. There is no need to use special finger paints exclusively, as the same effect can be had by spreading ordinary powder paint on a piece of polythene, ready for the children to draw the required pattern in the paint. The pattern can then be printed off.

Glue painting

Another idea which helps children with their perception as well as their fine motor control is to paint a pattern using glue, along which the children lay a piece of wool or string. Some teachers provide a washing-up liquid bottle containing fairly runny glue so that the children themselves can create the glue pattern before placing the wool or else spreading sand over the trails. Once the children have gained confidence in these approaches, which require no grip upon an implement, they are encouraged to use an implement of some sort to develop the pattern further. The chosen pattern is either on display, ready for copying, or shown to the children so that they have to repeat it from memory. This is a very important activity for spelling. When using the obvious medium of paint and brush, it is advisable to add washing-up liquid to the powder paint in order to encourage flow. If the flow is missing then the natural movement from left to right is destroyed, which can be rather inhibiting for the children.

Tracing

The following ideas are variations on a theme of tracing:

1. Place a piece of polythene or Perspex over the required pattern. This provides an element of tracing as well as helping with the problem of flow.

2. Patterns can be drawn on both sugar paper and chalk boards. As a writing implement, chalk closely resembles the pencil and it has a good level of resistance which helps children to feel the flow.

3. By using an overhead projector, it is possible to project patterns on to some object with a pale background which has a large piece of tracing paper spread over it. The children can then trace the patterns that are projected on to the tracing paper. This is a useful way not only to introduce the vertical plane to young children, in preparation for chalkboard work, but also to provide large patterns in order to encourage gross motor movements.

4. The above idea can be modified slightly to avoid the use of the projector. A large piece of card, with the required pattern drawn on it, is covered with a piece of polythene. The children then use a chinagraph or water-soluble pen to trace the pattern. Each tracing can be rubbed out ready for the next attempt.

   All of these ideas for large pattern work precede the fine motor activity of using a pencil. However, children should be encouraged to be involved in this work throughout the first year and often remedially. Indeed, the value of more sophisticated pattern work in art and craft must be considered alongside the learning of handwriting.

Pencil control

Once the children's fine motor skills begin to develop, the use of pencils, crayons, fibre-tip pens, etc. can be encouraged, alongside the continuation of the pre-writing skills.

Activities for enhancing pencil control will probably begin with free scribbling. In Fig. 16 are ideas for the teacher to keep in mind when preparing scribbling activities. These are <u>not</u> designed for tracing. Instead, the teacher might say, 'Put the hair on the face,' or 'Draw the smoke coming from the chimney.'

These ideas will lead to the more formal patterning found in *A Hand for Spelling*, Book 1.

Figure 16
Ideas for free scribbling

Drawing with channels

For this activity the teacher draws channels, in the form of parallel lines, which can then be duplicated on sheets of paper. The children are required to try to draw between the lines. The guidelines should be relatively simple at first: straight lines placed about 2 cm apart.

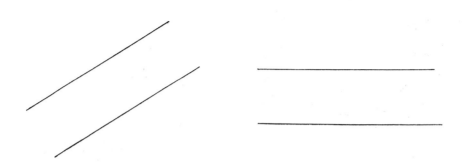

Later, the width may be reduced and then curved lines may be introduced to increase the difficulty.

The curved channels may gradually be modified into the shape of letters.
   A further idea using snakes is in *A Hand for Spelling* (see Fig. 17).

Figure 17
Snake letters

Mazes

The idea of 'channelling' can be extended to more complex mazes. These will provide an opportunity for problem-solving while helping children to develop muscular co-ordination and to improve their pen hold.

More formal handwriting patterns

The next stage is to provide more formal handwriting patterns which will foster the control required to form the flowing letter. It is worth remembering, however, that having to write the whole pattern across the page can be a problem and is likely to cause wrist tension. Allow for natural pen lifts which are a characteristic of writing. Also, it may be unwise to practise some patterns immediately prior to certain letters, as some children are likely to continue the pattern and fail to put in the ligature. For example, the pattern followed by a word with a double 'm', as in 'mummy', could cause difficulties.

When the children have reached the more formal stage of using a pencil, a handy record of development is to use one page of their books for a particular pattern. Ask the children to make the first attempt, at the top of the page. During the week there will be other opportunities to practise this pattern (perhaps in art and craft). The following week the improved attempt can be drawn at the bottom of the page (see Fig. 18).

Throughout any handwriting activity it is essential to ensure the following:

1. A correct pencil grip which is firm but relaxed. The writing implement should be held between thumb and index finger, resting against the middle finger. A triangular-shaped pencil will help any children who exhibit difficulties in holding the pencil correctly.

2. In order to help the flow of writing and to prevent children from pressing too hard on the paper, a 2B pencil is recommended.

3. Correct posture, namely sitting comfortably with feet flat on the floor and with body upright but tilted slightly forward on a chair that is suited to the height of the table.

4. Correct light in order to see the writing without eye strain.

5. The position of the paper should be adjusted to suit right- or left-handers, once the most comfortable writing position is found.

6. Provision must be made for left-handed children. If these children are taught *how to be left-handed* then they can write as freely and legibly as right-handed children.

Left-handed children

1. Left-handers must always sit to the left of a right-hander. This will avoid their arms colliding.

Figure 18
Pattern practice page

Date: _____

_____

/ week later

2. The left-hander must have the paper to the left of the mid-line of the body. After tilting the paper to a comfortable angle, it should be pushed about 5 cm away from the body. Incorrect paper position will usually result in an awkward, twisted grip. Some left-handers may need to hold the pencil a little further from the point than right-handers, so that the writing is not obscured by the thumb knuckle.

3. Left-handers need the light to come over their left shoulders.

4. It is also important for left-handers to sit on a higher chair. This higher position above the table, together with the paper being pushed away from the body, will prevent the elbow from locking into the side of the body when the writing has reached only half-way across the page.

5. Left-handers must be allowed to cross the letter 't' from right to left because, for a left-hander, this is a natural movement. The letter 'f' may also cause difficulties for left-handers if the cross stroke is used as the joining line.

The language of writing

Throughout all activities, the language of writing is crucial because it enables children to verbalise their physical actions and to understand the language that is used in the writing experience. Always use the letter names and not the sounds. Sounds can be used in reading but, when teaching letter strings, the use of sounds will lead to rhyming, which does not help the search for the correct letter string.

In addition to the letter names, the following words must also be taught:

top, bottom, up, down, round, over, back, letter, word, pattern, left, right, join, curved, straight, tall, short, long, horizontal, diagonal.

No doubt teachers will wish to add to this list.

Emphasis has already been placed on the need to talk through the letter shapes as they are first written. For example, the formation of a letter 'g' might be talked through like this: 'Start at one o'clock, come back and right round to one o'clock, straight down and down, curl round the little seat.' Teachers will discover their own language and indeed children will add to it. Some snappy groupings could be: the one o'clock club (c o a g d q), the down-back-up-again group (h r p m n b k), the stick team (j i x z). Ask the children for other groupings.

Flowing separate letters

At this stage the individual letters must be taught thoroughly, using a variety of media and techniques. A flowing letter is a letter that is formed in one movement, except for dots and cross strokes. Some letters have an exit ligature, for example, a, d, h. Logically, a joining line, which is an extension of a ligature, will follow. In developing the 'feel' for letters, use any or all of the following:

1. A writing finger in the air, sometimes with eyes closed.

2. Sandpaper letter shapes.

3. A shallow sand tray (ideal use for a jigsaw tray that is redundant). Write the letters with the writing finger. Simply shake the tray for a clean start.

4. *Roll 'n' Write* (LDA): rolling a ball bearing along a plastic track in the shape of a letter.

5. Snakes, as in *A Hand for Spelling* (LDA).

6. The use of the 'language of writing'.

7. A variety of writing implements, for example, pens, felt-tips.

8. Tracing over a letter (a highlighter pen is recommended for the teacher).

9. Writing letters from the same pattern group on top of one another. This helps to emphasise the basic shape, for example a, d, g.

Remember to observe carefully, since incorrect letter formation at this stage will cause untold problems later on. For teachers using *A Hand for Spelling*, it is vital to ensure that children have complete confidence in the writing of separate letters, through the above activities, before they are introduced to the letter strings which occur in Book 2.

Although letters can be taught according to their similarity of formation, they should also be taught in conjunction with the spelling programme. In other words, from as early as possible, children must learn to join together letters which belong to the spelling system, for example 'ag'. There is no need to master every one of the letters of the alphabet before practising letter strings. Moreover, it is not necessary to adhere to two-letter strings; letter strings containing three letters are often more significant. For example, 'ent' and 'ere' are very common, appearing in words such as 'went', 'here', 'there'.

A useful technique for establishing the correct motor movement is to encourage *overwriting* and then *underwriting* of the presented model, prior to challenging the children to write the whole letter string or word from memory. This strategy is employed throughout *A Hand for Spelling* (see Fig. 19).

Figure 19
Sample page of letter strings by a 5- year old

Name *Sean*

Trace over and then write the letter pattern

ea ea ea ea
ea ea ea ea

Now do the same with these words

eat sea seat meat
sea seat meat

each teach teacher
teacher

Cover each word and write it above the teacher.

teacher
seat
sea seat
meat

It is not suggested that capital letters are joined to lower case. They should be taught as a separate entity.

Introducing the writing of letters from memory

Children must be taught to look closely at letters and letter strings, such as 'ag', 'ere', 'ain', 'ome' etc. and then to write them without reference to the original image.
  The following ideas will help them to develop this technique:

1. Write the letter or letter string (which might be a word, for example, 'ant'). Discuss and look at it together before the children write it from memory.

2. Use an imaginary camera and photograph the word in your mind.

3. Draw it in the air with your eyes closed.

4. One child shows another child the letter, letter string, or word and then covers the image. After writing, they compare and discuss the result.

5. Write a word at the bottom of a paper strip. Fold over the paper and write the word again. The paper must be folded over before writing the word. Continue folding the paper and writing the word until reaching the top of the paper.

6. Overwrite, underwrite, and then turn over the paper and write the whole word from memory.

USE OF LINES

The literature on handwriting is equally divided regarding the use of lined or plain paper. At the early stage, however, plain paper is advocated because lines can inhibit the children's natural flow. Dots on either side of the paper will aid direction once the skill begins to develop. When the children develop a secure form, line guides may be used if desired.

TEACHING PRINT

The teaching of print must not be neglected. It can be introduced as 'art' by the time that children have reached lower junior age. If children are presented with a printed alphabet as a suitable model to follow, the skill is usually acquired very quickly. The role of the teacher will be to insist on its use at certain times, for example, as an art form, when making labels, or when annotating a diagram.

5

CONCLUSIONS

This final section draws on some of the comments from the schools that were mentioned in the Foreword regarding the teaching of joined writing to children on school entry over a period of three years.

Whilst their comments differed according to their teaching situation, there was no doubt that they all felt that they had been instrumental in helping many very young children to become more confident in their writing. In other words, they were convinced that the children, who had had the chance not only to develop a confident and flowing handwriting style but also to study the structure of words, were released to concentrate on the content of their writing. Consequently, there was a marked improvement in the quality of the children's written work, in all of the curriculum areas.

Many teachers said that they had for too long underestimated the ability of very young children. Others said that if they transferred to another school they would try very hard to persuade their new colleagues to change to a school policy with the following attributes:

1. A well-developed pre-writing programme that does not rush children into writing too early.

2. A great deal of discussion about the structure of words.

3. The introduction of flowing separate letters, followed by the joining of letter strings, from the beginning.

4. A formal approach to teaching these skills to ensure correct letter formation from the start.

5. A strong emphasis at the outset on the writing of letters and words from memory.

This resource book is intended to help teachers who are considering the introduction of joined writing to children on school entry but it must be emphasised that any change of practice is not easy. Teachers must beware of any ill-prepared launch into a curriculum initiative which not only expects children to change but also places heavy demands on teachers to change their own teaching style.

It was, however, quite evident that the teachers in the named schools had realised that changing their teaching style required a great deal of thought and additional effort. Now that it is part of their day-to-day practice, it is unlikely that they would wish to revert, especially when they consider the quality of free writing (see Fig. 20) that is produced by 5-year old children in their schools.

Figure 20
Free writing of a 5- year old

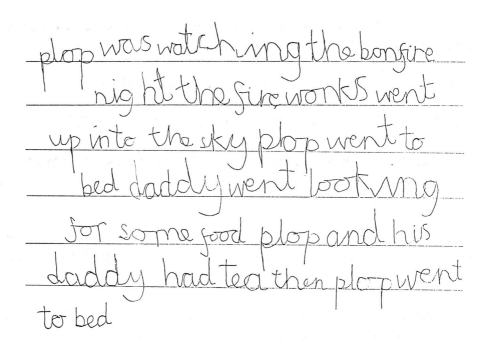

Bibliography

Alston, J. (1985) 'The Handwriting of Seven to Nine Year Olds', *British Journal of Special Education*: Vol 12: No 2.

Bennett, N., Desforges, C., Cockburn, A. and Wilkinson, B. (1985) *Quality of Learning Experience*, Croom Helm.

Clay, M. (1975) *What Did I Write?*, Heinemann.

Cripps, C. (1988) *A Hand for Spelling*, LDA.

Early, G. (1976) 'Cursive Handwriting, Reading and Spelling achievement', *Academic Therapy*: Paper 12.

Education, Ministry of (1959) *Primary Education: Suggestions for the Consideration of Teachers and Others Concerned with the Work of Primary Schools*, HMSO.

Education and Science, Department of (1982) *Education 5 to 9*, HMSO.

Education and Science, Department of (1984) *English from 5 to 16*, HMSO.

Education and Science, Department of et al. (1975) *A language for life: report of the Committee of Inquiry appointed by the Secretary of State for Education under the Chairmanship of Sir Alan Bullock*, HMSO.

Education and Science, Department of et al. (1988) *Report of the Committee of Inquiry in the teaching of English language appointed by the Secretary of State for Education under the Chairmanship of Sir John Kingman*, HMSO.

Education and Science, Department of Central Advisory Council for Education (England) (1963) *Children and their Primary Schools: a Report*, HMSO. (Plowden Report)

Education and Science, Department of and Welsh Office (1988) *English for ages 5 to 11: proposals of the Secretaries of State for Education and Science and for Wales*, London: DES.

Fairbank, A. (1970) *The Story of Handwriting*, Faber & Faber.

Fletcher, D.E. (1958) *Quick and Legible Handwriting*, Teachers' Manual, Oliver & Boyd.

Gelb, I.J. (1952) *A Study of Writing*, University of Chicago Press.

Gibson, E.J. and Levin, H. (1975) *The Psychology of Reading*, MIT Press.

Gray, N. (1977) 'Laying down the Letter', *Times Educational Supplement*, 19 Aug.

Hall, N. (1987) 'Printed on the Mind', *Child Education*, May.

Jarman, C. (1979) *The Development of Handwriting Skills*, Blackwell.

Mackay, D., Thompson, B. and Schuab, P. (1970) *Breakthrough to Literacy*, Longman for the Schools Council.

Marshack, A. (1975) 'Exploring the Mind of Ice Age Man', *The Occasional Journal of the National Geographic Society* 147.

Myers, P.W. (1983) 'Handwriting in English Education', *Visible Language* 17.

Oates, J. (1979) *Babylon*, Thames & Hudson.

Peters, M.L. (1985) *Spelling Caught or Taught: A New Look*, Routledge & Kegan Paul.

Richardson M. (1935) *Writing and Writing Patterns*, Hodder and Stoughton.

Sassoon, R. (1983) *The Practical Guide to Children's Handwriting*, Thames & Hudson.

Skipp, V. (1967) *Out of the Ancient World*, Oliver & Boyd.

Stanton, D. (1986) 'An Examination of the Relative Importance of Speed and Legibility in the Handwriting of Eleven-year old Children', Unpublished dissertation, Crewe and Alsager College of Higher Education.

A Hand For Spelling

A Hand For Spelling by Charles Cripps and also published by L.D.A. is the first resource to teach handwriting and spelling together. It contains over 500 photocopiable activities to take your pupils from pre-writing skills through letter formation to spelling at an eleven year old level.

Book 1 gives you 44 photocopy masters to develop pre-writing skills and letter formation. By completing 31 lively pictures, pupils learn to form the basic patterns essential to good letter formation, before moving on to the letters themselves. Friendly snakes show them where to start and finish each letter.

Book 2 gives you 92 photocopy masters dealing with words used by children aged 5 to 7. In book 2, pupils begin to join letters together, and have the opportunity to look at and write words that share the same letter patterns.

Book 3 builds on book 2, with another 92 photocopy masters which deal with words used by children aged 7 to 9. At this level, two exercises are presented on each page, and pupils begin to use the words to write sentences.

Book 4 gives you 92 photocopy masters which reinforce what has been learned in books 2 and 3, and introduce words used by children aged 9 to 11 to give pupils confidence with spelling at an eleven year old level.

For further details of *A Hand For Spelling* write to:
L.D.A., Duke Street, Wisbech, Cambridgeshire, PE13 2AE, or phone (0945) 63441.